SpringerBriefs in Computer Science

Series Editors

Stan Zdonik
Peng Ning
Shashi Shekhar
Jonathan Katz
Xindong Wu
Lakhmi C. Jain
David Padua
Xuemin Shen
Borko Furht
V. S. Subrahmanian

T0211616

For further volumes:
http://www.springer.com/series/10028

Cícero Nogueira dos Santos
Ruy Luiz Milidiú

Entropy Guided Transformation Learning: Algorithms and Applications

 Springer

Cícero Nogueira dos Santos
Research, IBM Research Brazil
Av. Pasteur 146
Rio de Janeiro, RJ
22296-903
Brazil

Ruy Luiz Milidiú
Departamento de Informática (DI)
Pontifícia Universidade Católica do
  Rio de Janeiro (PUC-Rio)
Rio de Janeiro, RJ
Brazil

ISSN 2191-5768
ISBN 978-1-4471-2977-6
DOI 10.1007/978-1-4471-2978-3
Springer London Heidelberg New York Dordrecht

e-ISSN 2191-5776
e-ISBN 978-1-4471-2978-3

British Library Cataloguing in Publication Data
A catalogue record for this book is available from the British Library

Library of Congress Control Number: 2012933839

Printed on acid-free paper

Springer is part of Springer Science+Business Media (www.springer.com)

Preface

This book presents entropy guided transformation learning (ETL), a machine learning algorithm for classification tasks. ETL generalizes transformation based learning (TBL) by automatically solving the TBL bottleneck: the construction of good template sets. ETL uses the Information Gain measure, through Decision Trees induction, in order to select the feature combinations that provide good template sets. This book also details ETL Committee, an ensemble method that uses ETL as the base learner.

The main advantage of ETL is its easy applicability to natural language processing (NLP) tasks. Its modeling phase is quick and simple. It only requires a training set and a naive initial classifier. Moreover, ETL inherits the TBL flexibility to work with diverse feature types. We also show that ETL can use the template evolution strategy to accelerate transformation learning.

The book also details the application of ETL to four language independent NLP tasks: part-of-speech tagging, phrase chunking, named entity recognition and semantic role labeling. Overall, we apply it to thirteen different corpora in six different languages: Dutch, English, German, Hindi, Portuguese and Spanish. Our extensive experimental results demonstrate that ETL is an effective way to learn accurate transformation rules. Using a common parameter setting, ETL shows better results than TBL with handcrafted templates for the four tasks. For the Portuguese language, ETL obtains state-of-the-art results for all tested corpora. Our experimental results also show that ETL Committee improves the effectiveness of ETL classifiers. Using the ETL Committee approach, we obtain state-of-the-art competitive performance results in the thirteen corpus-driven tasks. We believe that by avoiding the use of handcrafted templates, ETL enables the use of transformation rules to a greater range of NLP tasks.

The text provides a comprehensive introduction to ETL and its NLP applications. It is suitable for advanced undergraduate or graduate courses in Machine Learning and Natural Language Processing.

Rio de Janeiro, January 2012   Ruy L. Milidiú

Acknowledgments

We would like to express our gratitude to the National Council for Scientific and Technological Development (CNPq) for the financial support, without which this work would not have been realized.

We are thankful to the PUC–Rio's Postgraduate Program in Informatics for providing an excellent academic environment.

We would like to thank Professors Bianca Zadrozny, Daniel Schwabe, Fernando Carvalho, Raúl Renteria and Violeta Quental, for their beneficial comments and critiques.

Contents

Acronyms

CoNLL	Conference on Computational Natural Language Learning
CRF	Conditional random fields
DT	Decision trees
ETL	Entropy guided transformation learning
HAREM	Evaluation contest for named entity recognition in Portuguese
HMM	Hidden markov models
IG	Information gain
ML	Machine learning
NER	Named entity recognition
NLP	Natural language processing
NP	Noun phrase
PCK	Phrase chunking
POS	Part-of-speech
PROPOR	International conference on computational processing of Portuguese
TBL	Transformation based learning
SPSAL	Workshop on shallow parsing for south Asian languages
SRL	Semantic role labeling
SVM	Support vector machines

Part I
Entropy Guided Transformation Learning: Algorithms

Chapter 1
Introduction

Abstract This chapter presents a brief introduction to entropy guided transformation learning (ETL), a machine learning algorithm for classification tasks. ETL generalizes transformation based learning (TBL) by automatically solving the TBL bottleneck: the construction of good template sets. The main advantage of ETL is its easy applicability to natural language processing (NLP) tasks. This introductory chapter presents the motivation behind ETL and summarizes our experimental results. In Sect. 1.1, we first briefly detail TBL and explain its bottleneck. Next, we briefly present ETL and list some of its advantages. In Sect. 1.2, we first list some related works on the use of ETL for different NLP tasks. Next, we report a summary of our experimental results on the application of ETL to four language independent NLP tasks: part-of-speech tagging, phrase chunking, named entity recognition and semantic role labeling. Finally, in Sect. 1.3, we detail the structure of the book.

Keywords Machine learning · Entropy guided transformation learning · ETL committee · Transformation based learning · Natural language processing · Part-of-speech tagging · Phrase chunking · Named entity recognition · Semantic role labeling

1.1 Motivation

Transformation based learning is a machine learning (ML) algorithm for classification tasks introduced by Brill [2]. TBL is a corpus-based, error-driven approach that learns a set of ordered transformation rules which correct mistakes of a baseline classifier. It has been used for several natural language processing tasks such as part-of-speech tagging [2, 8, 15], phrase chunking [9, 22, 27, 28], spelling correction [21], appositive extraction [17], named entity recognition [16, 24], semantic role labeling [18], semantic parsing [20], predicate argument structure analysis [33] and text summarization [29].

C. N. dos Santos and R. L. Milidiú, *Entropy Guided Transformation Learning*: *Algorithms and Applications*, SpringerBriefs in Computer Science, DOI: 10.1007/978-1-4471-2978-3_1, © The Author(s) 2012

TBL rules must follow patterns, called templates, that are meant to capture the relevant feature combinations. TBL rule templates are handcrafted by problem experts. Its quality strongly depends on the problem expert skills to build them. Even when a template set is available for a given task, it may not be effective when we change from a language to another. Moreover, when the number of features to be considered is large, the effort to manually create templates is extremely increased, becoming sometimes infeasible. Hence, the human driven construction of good template sets is a bottleneck on the effective use of the TBL approach.

In this book, we present entropy guided transformation learning, a machine learning algorithm that generalizes TBL. ETL solves the TBL bottleneck by using the Information Gain measure, through decision trees induction, to select the feature combinations that provide good template sets. This book also details ETL committee, an ensemble method that uses ETL as the base learner. ETL committee relies on the use of training data manipulation to create an ensemble of classifiers.

The main advantage of ETL is its easy applicability to natural language processing tasks. Its modeling phase is quick and simple. It only requires a training set and a naive initial classifier. Moreover, ETL inherits the TBL flexibility to work with diverse feature types and also provides an effective way to handle high dimensional features. ETL enables the inclusion of the *current classification* feature in the generated templates. We also show that ETL can use the *template evolution* strategy [3] to accelerate transformation learning.

1.2 Applications

Since its introduction by Santos and Milidiú [5], ETL has been successfully applied to a broad range of NLP tasks. Some of these tasks include part-of-speech (POS) tagging [6, 8], phrase chunking (PCK) [6, 7, 25, 26], clause identification [12, 14], named entity recognition (NER) [6, 7, 26], semantic role labeling (SRL) [7], dependency parsing [23], hedge detection [11], quotation extraction [10] and coreference resolution [4]. Additionally, in a very short period of time, ETL allowed the creation of F-EXT-WS [13], a web based Natural Language Processor. For the Portuguese language, this web service provides the processing of various tasks such as POS tagging, PCK and NER. In [1], F-EXT-WS is used to generate features for sentiment analysis of financial news.

In this book, we detail the application of ETL to four language independent NLP tasks: part-of-speech tagging, phrase chunking, named entity recognition and semantic role labeling. POS tagging is the process of assigning a POS or another lexical class marker to each word in a text [19]. PCK consists in dividing a text into non-overlapping phrases [30]. NER is the problem of finding all proper nouns in a text and to classify them among several given categories of interest [24]. SRL is the process of detecting basic event structures such as *who* did *what* to *whom*, *when* and *where* [32]. These tasks have been considered fundamental for more advanced NLP applications [30, 31, 34, 35]. Overall, we apply ETL to thirteen different corpora

Table 1.1 Corpus characteristics

Task	Corpus	Language	Sentences	Tokens
POS	Mac-Morpho	Portuguese	53,374	1,221,465
	Tycho Brahe	Portuguese	40,932	1,035,592
	Brown	English	57,340	1,161,192
	TIGER	German	50,474	888,578
PCK	SNR-CLIC	Portuguese	4,392	104,144
	Ramshaw and Marcus	English	10,948	259,104
	CoNLL-2000	English	10,948	259,104
	SPSAL-2007	Hindi	1,134	25,000
NER	HAREM	Portuguese	8,142	165,102
	SPA CoNLL-2002	Spanish	9,840	316,248
	DUT CoNLL-2002	Dutch	21,001	271,925
SRL	CoNLL-2004	English	10,607	251,766
	CoNLL-2005	English	42,248	1,006,712

Table 1.2 System performances

Task	Corpus	State-of-the-art		ETL	
		System	Performance	Single	Committee
POS	Mac-Morpho	TBL	96.60	96.75	**96.94**
	Tycho Brahe	TBL	96.63	96.64	**96.72**
	Brown	TBL	96.67	96.69	**96.83**
	TIGER	TBL	96.53	96.57	**96.68**
PCK	SNR-CLIC	TBL	87.71	88.85	**89.58**
	Ramshaw and Marcus	SVM	**94.22**	92.80	93.29
	CoNLL-2000	SVM	**94.12**	92.28	93.27
	SPSAL-2007	HMM + CRF	**80.97**	78.53	80.44
NER	HAREM	CORTEX	61.57	61.32	**63.56**
	SPA CoNLL-2002	AdaBoost	**79.29**	76.28	77.46
	DUT CoNLL-2002	AdaBoost	**77.05**	74.18	75.44
SRL	CoNLL-2004	SVM	**69.49**	63.37	67.39
	CoNLL-2005	AdaBoost	**75.47**	70.08	72.23

in six different languages: Dutch, English, German, Hindi, Portuguese and Spanish. Our goal in these experiments is to assess the robustness and predictive power of the ETL strategy.

In Table 1.1, we enumerate the thirteen corpora used throughout this work. For each corpus, we indicate its corresponding language, task and size. The reported size is in terms of sentences and tokens. A *token* is a word or a punctuation mark. In our experiments, a common ETL parameter setting is used for the four tasks.

In Table 1.2, we summarize, for each corpus, the performance of both ETL and the state-of-the-art system. The performance measure for the POS tagging task is accuracy. For the other three tasks, the performance measure is the $F_{\beta = 1}$. In Table 1.2, the best observed results are in bold. Using the ETL approach, we obtain competitive performance results for the thirteen corpora. For each one of the tasks, ETL shows better results than TBL with handcrafted templates. ETL committee improves the effectiveness of ETL classifiers in all cases and achieves state-of-the-art results for six corpora. Chapters 5 through 8 describe our experiments and results.

1.3 Overview of the Book

The remainder of the book is organized as follows. In Chap. 2, the ETL algorithm is detailed. In Chap. 3, we describe an effective method to create ETL committees. In Chap. 4, we show the general ETL modeling for NLP tasks. In Chap. 5, we report our findings on the application of ETL to POS tagging. In Chap. 6, we detail the application of ETL to the PCK task. In Chap. 7, we report our findings on the application of ETL to the NER task. In Chap. 8, we detail the application of ETL to the SRL task. Finally, in Chap. 9, we present our concluding remarks and future work.

References

1. Alvim, L., Vilela, P., Motta, E., Milidiú, R.L.: Sentiment of financial news: a natural language processing approach. In: 1st Workshop on Natural Language Processing Tools Applied to Discourse Analysis in Psychology, Buenos Aires (2010)
2. Brill, E.: Transformation-based error-driven learning and natural language processing: a case study in part-of-speech tagging. Comput. Linguist. **21**(4), 543–565 (1995)
3. Curran, J.R., Wong, R.K.: Formalisation of transformation-based learning. In: Proceedings of the ACSC, pp. 51–57, Canberra (2000)
4. dos Santos, C.N., Carvalho, D.L.: Rule and tree ensembles for unrestricted coreference resolution. In: Proceedings of the Fifteenth Conference on Computational Natural Language Learning: Shared Task, pp. 51–55. Association for Computational Linguistics, Portland (2011). http://www.aclweb.org/anthology/W11-1906
5. dos Santos, C.N., Milidiú, R.L.: Entropy guided transformation learning. Technical Report 29/07, Departamento de Informática, PUC-Rio (2007). http://bib-di.inf.puc-rio.br/techreports/2007.htm
6. dos Santos, C.N., Milidiú, R.L.: Entropy guided transformation learning. In: Hassanien, A.E., Abraham, A., Vasilakos, A.V., Pedrycz, W. (eds.) Learning and Approximation: Theoretical Foundations and Applications, Foundations of Computational Intelligence, vol. 1. Springer, Berlin (2009)
7. dos Santos, C.N., Milidiú, R.L., Crestana, C.E.M., Fernandes, E.R.: ETL ensembles for chunking, NER and SRL. In: Proceedings of the 11th International Conference on Intelligent Text Processing and Computational Linguistics—CICLing, pp. 100–112 (2010)
8. dos Santos, C.N., Milidiú, R.L., Rentería, R.P.: Portuguese part-of-speech tagging using entropy guided transformation learning. In: Proceedings of 8th Workshop on Computational Processing of Written and Spoken Portuguese, pp. 143–152, Aveiro (2008)
9. dos Santos, C.N., Oliveira, C.: Constrained atomic term: widening the reach of rule templates in transformation based learning. In: Portuguese Conference on Artificial Intelligence—EPIA, pp. 622–633 (2005)

10. Fernandes, E., Milidiú, R.L., Rentería, R.: Relhunter: a machine learning method for relation extraction from text. J. Braz. Comput. Soc. **16**, 191–199 (2010). doi:10.1007/s13173-010-0018-y
11. Fernandes, E.R., Crestana, C.E.M., Milidiú, R.L.: Hedge detection using the Relhunter approach. In: Farkas, R., Vincze, V., Szarvas, G., Móra, G., Csirik, J. (eds.) Proceedings of the Fourteenth Conference on Computational Natural Language Learning: Shared Task, pp. 64–69. Association for Computational Linguistics, Stroudsburg (2010)
12. Fernandes, E.R., Pires, B.A., dos Santos, C.N., Milidiú, R.L.: Clause identification using entropy guided transformation learning. In: Proceedings of 7th Brazilian Symposium in Information and Human Language Technology (2009)
13. Fernandes, E.R., dos Santos, C.N., Milidiú, R.L.: Portuguese language processing service. In: Proceedings of the WWW in Ibero-America Alternate Track of the 19th International World Wide Web Conference (2009)
14. Fernandes, E.R., dos Santos, C.N., Milidiú, R.L.: A machine learning approach to portuguese clause identification. In: Proceedings of the International Conference on Computational Processing of Portuguese, Language, pp. 55–64 (2010)
15. Finger, M.: Técnicas de otimização da precisão empregadas no etiquetador tycho brahe. In: Proceedings of the Workshop on Computational Processing of Written and Spoken Portuguese, pp. 141–154, São Paulo (2000)
16. Florian, R.: Named entity recognition as a house of cards: classifier stacking. In: Proceedings of CoNLL-2002, pp. 175–178, Taipei (2002)
17. Freitas, M.C., Duarte, J.C., dos Santos, C.N., Milidiú, R.L., Renteria, R.P., Quental, V.: A machine learning approach to the identification of appositives. In: Proceedings of Ibero-American AI Conference—IBERAMIA, Ribeirão Preto (2006)
18. Higgins, D.: A transformation-based approach to argument labeling. In: Ng, H.T., Riloff, E. (eds.) HLT-NAACL 2004 Workshop: Eighth Conference on Computational Natural Language Learning (CoNLL-2004), pp. 114–117. Association for Computational Linguistics, Boston (2004)
19. Jurafsky, D., Martin, J.H.: Speech and Language Processing. Prentice Hall, Upper Saddle River (2000)
20. Jurcícek, F., Gasic, M., Keizer, S., Mairesse, F., Thomson, B., Yu, K., Young, S.: Transformation-based learning for semantic parsing. In: INTERSPEECH, pp. 2719–2722 (2009)
21. Mangu, L., Brill, E.: Automatic rule acquisition for spelling correction. In: Fisher, D.H. (ed.) Proceedings of The Fourteenth ICML. Morgan Kaufmann, San Francisco (1997)
22. Megyesi, B.: Shallow parsing with pos taggers and linguistic features. J. Mach. Learn. Res. **2**, 639–668 (2002)
23. Milidiú, R.L., Crestana, C.E.M., dos Santos, C.N.: A token classification approach to dependency parsing. In: Proceedings of 7th Brazilian Symposium in Information and Human Language Technology (2009)
24. Milidiú, R.L., Duarte, J.C., Cavalcante, R.: Machine learning algorithms for portuguese named entity recognition. In: Proceedings of Fourth Workshop in Information and Human Language Technology, Ribeirão Preto (2006)
25. Milidiú, R.L., dos Santos, C.N., Duarte, J.C.: Phrase chunking using entropy guided transformation learning. In: Proceedings of the 46th Annual Meeting of the Association for Computational Linguistics: Human Language Technologies—ACL-08: HLT, Columbus (2008)
26. Milidiú, R.L., dos Santos, C.N., Duarte, J.C.: Portuguese corpus-based learning using ETL. J. Braz. Comput. Soc. **14**(4), 17–27 (2008)
27. Milidiú, R.L., dos Santos, C.N., Duarte, J.C., Renteria, R.P.: Semi-supervised learning for portuguese noun phrase extraction. In: Proceedings of 7th Workshop on Computational Processing of Written and Spoken Portuguese, pp. 200–203, Itatiaia (2006)
28. Ramshaw, L., Marcus, M.: Text chunking using transformation-based learning. In: Armstrong, S., Church, K., Isabelle, P., Manzi, S., Tzoukermann, E., Yarowsky, D. (eds.) Natural Language Processing Using Very Large Corpora. Kluwer, Dordrecht (1999)

29. Saggion, H.: Learning predicate insertion rules for document abstracting. In: 12th International Conference on Computational Linguistics and Intelligent Text Processing, pp. 301–312 (2011)
30. Sang, E.F.T.K., Buchholz, S.: Introduction to the CoNLL-2000 shared task: chunking. In: Proceedings of the 2nd Workshop on Learning Language in Logic and the 4th CoNLL, pp. 127–132. Association for Computational Linguistics, Morristown (2000). doi:10.3115/1117601.1117631
31. Surdeanu, M., Johansson, R., Meyers, A., Màrquez, L., Nivre, J.: The CoNLL 2008 shared task on joint parsing of syntactic and semantic dependencies. In: CoNLL 2008: Proceedings of the Twelfth Conference on Computational Natural Language Learning, pp. 159–177. Coling 2008 Organizing Committee, Manchester (2008). http://www.aclweb.org/anthology/W08-2121
32. Surdeanu, M., Màrquez, L., Carreras, X., Comas, P.: Combination strategies for semantic role labeling. J. Artif. Intell. Res. **29**, 105–151 (2007)
33. Taira, H., Fujita, S., Nagata, M.: Predicate argument structure analysis using transformation-based learning. In: Hajič, J., Carberry, S., Clark, S., Nivre, J. (eds.) Proceedings of the ACL 2010 Conference Short Papers, ACLShort '10, pp. 162–167. Association for Computational Linguistics, Stroudsburg (2010)
34. Tjong Kim Sang, E.F.: Introduction to the CoNLL-2002 shared task: language-independent named entity recognition. In: Roth, D., van den Bosch, A. (eds.) Proceedings of CoNLL-2002, pp. 155–158, Taipei (2002)
35. Tjong Kim Sang, E.F., De Meulder, F.: Introduction to the CoNLL-2003 shared task: language-independent named entity recognition. In: Daelemans, W., Osborne, M. (eds.) Proceedings of CoNLL-2003, pp. 142–147. Edmonton, Canada (2003)

Chapter 2
Entropy Guided Transformation Learning

Abstract This chapter details the entropy guided transformation learning algorithm [8, 23]. ETL is an effective way to overcome the transformation based learning bottleneck: the construction of good template sets. In order to better motivate and describe ETL, we first provide an overview of the TBL algorithm in Sect. 2.1. Next, in Sect. 2.2, we explain why the manual construction of template sets is a bottleneck for TBL. Then, in Sect. 2.3, we detail the entropy guided template generation strategy employed by ETL. In Sect. 2.3, we also present strategies to handle high dimensional features and to include the current classification feature in the generated templates. In Sects. 2.4–2.6 we present some variations on the basic ETL strategy. Finally, in Sect. 2.7, we discuss some related works.

Keywords Machine learning · Entropy guided transformation learning · Transformation based learning · Information gain · Decision trees · Transformation rules · Feature selection

2.1 Transformation Based Learning

Transformation based learning is a supervised ML algorithm usually applied to NLP tasks. TBL generates a set of transformation rules that correct classification mistakes of a baseline classifier [3]. The following three rules illustrate the kind of transformation rules learned by TBL.

$$pos[0] = ART \quad pos[1] = ART \rightarrow pos[0] = PREP$$
$$pos[0] = ART \quad pos[1] = V \quad word[0] = a \rightarrow pos[0] = PREP$$
$$pos[0] = N \quad pos[-1] = N \quad pos[-2] = ART \rightarrow pos[0] = ADJ$$

These rules were learned for Portuguese POS tagging. They check the following features: $pos[0]$, the POS tag of the current word; $pos[1]$, the POS tag of the next word; $pos[-1]$, the POS tag of the previous word; $pos[-2]$, the POS tag of

C. N. dos Santos and R. L. Milidiú, *Entropy Guided Transformation Learning:*
Algorithms and Applications, SpringerBriefs in Computer Science,
DOI: 10.1007/978-1-4471-2978-3_2, © The Author(s) 2012

Fig. 2.1 Transformation
based learning

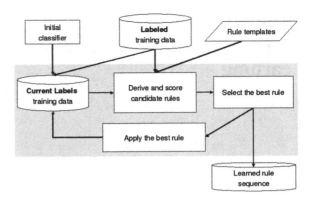

the word two before; and `word[0]`, the current lexical item. The first rule should
be read as

> "**IF** the POS tag of the current word is an *article*
> **AND** the POS tag of the next word is an *article*
> **THEN** change the POS tag of the current word to *preposition*"

TBL rules are composed of two parts: the left hand side and the right hand side.
The *left hand side* is a conjunction of feature = value tests, whereas the *right hand
side* indicates a value assignment to a target feature. TBL rules must follow patterns,
called *rule templates*, that specify which feature combinations should appear in the
rule left-hand side. The template set defines the candidate rules space to be searched.
Briefly, a template is an uninstantiated rule. The following three templates were used
to create the previously shown rules.

```
pos[0] pos[1]
pos[0] pos[1]   word[0]
pos[0] pos[-1]  pos[-2]
```

TBL requires three main inputs:

(i) a correctly labeled training set;
(ii) an initial (baseline) classifier, the *baseline system* (BLS), which provides an
initial labeling for the training examples. Usually, the BLS is based on simple
statistics of the correctly labeled training set, such as to apply the most frequent
class;
(iii) a set of rule templates.

The TBL algorithm is illustrated in Fig. 2.1. The central idea in the TBL learning
process is to greedily learn rules that incrementally reduces the number of classification errors produced by the initial classifier. At each iteration, the algorithm learns
the rule that has the highest *score*. The score of a rule r is the difference between the
number of errors that r repairs and the number of errors that r creates. The learning

process stops when there are no more rules whose score is above a given threshold. The *rule score threshold* is a parameter of TBL.

A pseudo-code of TBL is presented in Algorithm 1. In this pseudo-code, the *apply* function classifies the given training set examples using the given initial classifier or transformation rule. The *isWronglyClassified* function checks whether the example is misclassified or not. This checking is done by comparing the current example class to the correct class. The *instantiateRule* function creates a new rule by instantiating the given template with the given example context values. The *countCorrections* function returns the number of corrections that a given rule would produce in the current training set. Similarly, the *countErrors* function returns the number of mis-classifications that a given rule would produce in the current training set. There are also several variants of the TBL algorithm. FastTBL [14] is the most successful, since it achieves a significant speedup in the training time while still achieving the same performance as the standard TBL algorithm. We have also developed a TBL variant that produces probabilistic classifications [9].

When using a TBL rule set to classify new data, we first apply the Initial Classifier to the new data. Then we apply the learned rule sequence. The rules must be applied following the same order they were learned.

2.2 TBL Bottleneck

TBL templates are meant to capture relevant feature combinations. Templates are handcrafted by problem experts. Therefore, TBL templates are task specific and their quality strongly depends on the problem expert skills to build them. For instance, Ramshaw and Marcus [29] propose a set of 100 templates for the phrase chunking task. Florian [12] proposes a set of 133 templates for the named entity recognition task. Higgins [16] handcrafted 130 templates to solve the semantic role labeling task. Elming [11] handcrafted 70 templates when applying TBL for machine translation.

The development of effective template sets is a difficult task. It usually involves a lengthy trial-and-error strategy or the adaptation of an existent, known-to-perform-well-on-a-similar-task template set to the new task [13]. The template developer should indicate the relevant feature combinations, otherwise the TBL algorithm can not learn effective rules. When the number of features to be considered is large, the effort to manually combine them is extremely increased, since there are $2^{|\mathscr{F}|}$ feature combinations, where $\mathscr{F}$ denotes the feature set. On the other hand, the template developer can not generate a very large number of templates, since the training time and memory requirements become intractable. Moreover, Ramshaw and Marcus [28] argue that overfitting is likely when irrelevant templates are included. *Overfitting* is the phenomenon of training too complex a model that do not generalize for new data.

Algorithm 1 Transformation Based Learning Pseudo-Code

input *LabeledTrainingSet*; *TemplateSet*;
    InitialClassifier; *RuleScoreThreshold*
1: *LearnedRules* ← {}
2: *CurrentTrainingSet* ← apply(*InitialClassifier*, *LabeledTrainingSet*)
3: **repeat**
4:   *CandidateRules* ← {}
5:   **for all** *example* ∈ *CurrentTrainingSet* **do**
6:     **if** isWronglyClassified(*example*) **then**
7:       **for all** *template* ∈ *TemplateSet* **do**
8:         *rule* ← instantiateRule(*template*, *example*)
9:         *CandidateRules* ← *CandidateRules* + *rule*
10:       **end for**
11:     **end if**
12:   **end for**
13:   *bestScore* ← 0
14:   *bestRule* ← Null
15:   **for all** *rule* ∈ *CandidateRules* **do**
16:     *good* ← countCorrections(*rule*, *CurrentTrainingSet*)
17:     *bad* ← countErrors(*rule*, *CurrentTrainingSet*)
18:     *score* ← *good* − *bad*
19:     **if** *score* > *bestScore* **then**
20:       *bestScore* ← *score*
21:       *bestRule* ← *rule*
22:     **end if**
23:   **end for**
24:   **if** *bestScore* > *RuleScoreThreshold* **then**
25:     *CurrentTrainingSet* ← apply(*bestRule*, *CurrentTrainingSet*)
26:     *LearnedRules* ← *LearnedRules* + *bestRule*
27:   **end if**
28: **until** *bestScore* > *RuleScoreThreshold*
output *LearnedRules*

Even when a template set is available for a given task, it may not be effective when we change from a language to another. For instance, dos Santos and Oliveira [10] extend the Ramshaw and Marcus [29] template set, which was handcrafted for English phrase chunking, by adding six templates specifically designed for Portuguese phrase chunking.

Based on the above, it can be concluded that the human driven construction of good template sets is a bottleneck on the effective use of the TBL approach.

2.3 Entropy Guided Template Generation

The main propose of ETL is to overcome the TBL bottleneck. In this section, we explain the strategy for automatic template generation employed by ETL. The template generation process is *entropy guided*. It uses information gain (IG) in order to select the feature combinations that provide good template sets. IG, which is based

Fig. 2.2 Entropy
guided transformation
learning

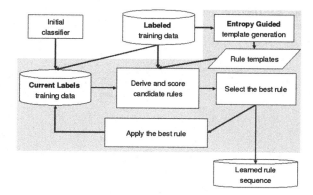

on the data entropy, is a key measure for many feature selection strategies. The ETL
algorithm is illustrated in the Fig. 2.2.

The template generation strategy employed by ETL uses decision trees (DT)
induction to obtain entropy guided feature selection. The most popular DT learning
algorithms [27, 30] use the IG measure in their feature selection step. Moreover,
most DT induction algorithms are efficient in terms of CPU and memory usage
[30]. Hence, they provide a quick way to obtain entropy guided feature selection.
However, DT algorithms that use IG are usually ineffective to deal with high dimensional features. Therefore, in ETL, we developed an effective way to handle high
dimensional features. ETL also enables the inclusion of the *current classification*
feature in the generated templates. This kind of feature, which changes during the
learning process, is not used in ML algorithms like DTs.

The remainder of this section is organized as follows. First, we review the IG
measure and the DT learning method. Next, we show how to automatically generate
templates from decision trees. Next, we present the ETL true class trick, which
enables the generation of templates that use the *current classification* feature. Finally,
we detail how ETL handles high dimensional features.

2.3.1 Information Gain

Information gain is a statistical measure commonly used to assess feature relevance
[7, 15, 26]. IG is based on the Entropy concept, which characterizes the impurity of
an arbitrary collection of examples. Given a training set T whose examples assume
classes from the set C. The entropy of T relative to this classification is defined as

$$H(T) = -\sum_{i=1}^{|C|} P_T(c_i) \log_2 P_T(c_i) \tag{2.1}$$

Fig. 2.3 Decision tree
learning

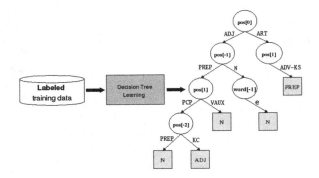

where c_i is a class label from C, $|C|$ is the number of classes and $P_T(c_i)$ is estimated
by the percentage of examples belonging to c_i in T.

In feature selection, information gain can be thought as the expected reduction in
entropy $H(T)$ caused by using a given feature A to partition the training examples
in T. The information gain $IG(T, A)$ of a feature A, relative to an example set T is
defined as

$$IG(T, A) = H(T) - \sum_{v \in Values(A)} \frac{|T_v|}{|T|} H(T_v) \qquad (2.2)$$

where $Values(A)$ is the set of all possible values for feature A, and T_v is the subset
of T for which feature A has value v [24]. When using information gain for feature
selection, a feature A is preferred to feature B if the information gain from A is
greater than that from B.

2.3.2 Decision Trees

Decision tree induction is a widely used machine learning algorithm [26]. Quinlan's
C4.5 [27] system is the most popular DT induction implementation. It recursively
partitions the training set using the feature providing the largest information gain.
This results into a tree structure, where the nodes correspond to the selected features
and the arc labels to the selected feature values. After the tree is grown, a pruning
step is carried out in order to avoid overfitting.

In Fig. 2.3, we illustrate the DT induction process for Portuguese POS tagging.
Here, the five selected features are: pos[0], the POS tag of the current word;
pos[−1], the POS tag of the previous word; pos[1], the POS tag of the next
word; pos[−2], the POS tag of the word two before; and word[−1], the previous
lexical item. The feature values are shown in the figure as arc labels.

We use the C4.5 system to obtain the required entropy guided selected features.
We use pruned trees in all experiments shown here.

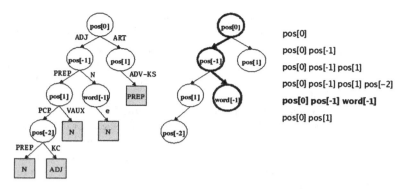

Fig. 2.4 Decision tree template extraction

2.3.3 Template Extraction

In a DT, the more informative features appear closer to the root. Since we just want to generate the most promising templates, we combine first the more informative features. Hence, as we traverse the DT from the root to a leaf, we collect the features in this path. This feature combination provides an information gain driven template. Additionally, paths from the root to internal nodes also provide good templates.

It is very simple to obtain these templates from C4.5's output. From the given DT, we eliminate the leaves and the arc labels. We keep only the tree structure and the node labels. Next, we execute a depth-first traversal of the DT. For each visited tree node, we create a template that combines the features in the path from the root to this node. Figure 2.4 illustrates the template extraction process. In this figure, the template in bold is extracted from the tree path in bold.

2.3.4 True Class Trick

TBL learning can access intermediate results of the classification process as a feature. Moreover, due to the iterative nature of the error correction approach adopted by TBL, the information in the *current classification feature* becomes more precise throughout the rule application process. For instance, when applying TBL to NLP tasks, one usual feature is the current classification of the words within a context window. This behavior is very desirable for NLP tasks, where local classification dependencies play an important role. In order to explore this TBL property in the ETL approach, the current classification feature must be available for selection in the template generation process. We include this feature by providing the DT learner with the initial and true classification of the words. We call this strategy as the *true class trick*.

When creating DT examples, we use the following information as the value of the current classification features: (1) the initial class label for the target word; and (2) the true class label for the neighbor words. Using the true class labels for the neighbor words produce better results, since they contain a precise information. This reflects what the TBL algorithm finds in the context window after some iterations. At this point, the total number of remaining errors is small, dispersed and spread throughout the data. Hence, around an incorrectly classified word is very likely that all the words are correctly classified. Using the true class labels for the target word is not allowed, since it would imply the use of the task solution as an input feature.

The use of the true class labels at training time is a general modeling strategy. It is usual for algorithms that do not have access to intermediate classification results, such as DT and support vector machines (SVM). For instance, when training an AdaBoost system for SRL, Surdeanu et al. [31] use the true class labels of the left side words. At test time, they use the class labels predicted by the classifier, since the classification is done in a left to right fashion. Kudo and Matsumoto [19] use a similar strategy when applying SVM for Phrase Chunking. The advantage of TBL over these algorithms is that, by default, it has access to the current classification of the words in both left and right sides, both at training and at test time. Furthermore, the ETL *true class trick* allows the effective use of this TBL property.

2.3.5 High Dimensional Features

High dimensional features are characterized by having a large number of possible values. For instance, the feature *words* in a text is high dimensional, since it can assume thousands of different values. This kind of feature is ineffective when information gain is used as the feature informativeness measure. IG has a bias that favors high dimensional features over those with a few values [24]. Since we use information gain in the ETL method, through DT learning, we must overcome this problem.

Although the C4.5 system uses the IG ratio measure to avoid the IG bias, the use of high dimensional features is still ineffective. When these features are present in the training set, usually the C4.5 system does not make use of them. Therefore, we include a preprocessing step. This step consists in pruning the high dimensional features in order to retain only their most informative values.

Let T be a training set that contains the high dimensional feature A. For each value v that A assumes in T, we compute its individual information gain using the following equation.

$$IG(T, A, v) = H(T) - \frac{|T_v|}{|T|} H(T_v) \qquad (2.3)$$

where $H(T)$ is the entropy of the training set T, T_v is the subset of T for which feature A has value v, and $H(T_v)$ is the entropy of the subset T_v. After the individual IGs are computed, we sort the feature values in decreasing order of IG. Let SV be

Table 2.1 ETL Template
evolution

Phase	Template set
1	pos [0]
2	pos [0] pos [−1]
	pos [0] pos [1]
3	pos [0] pos [−1] pos [1]
	pos [0] pos [−1] word [−1]
4	pos [0] pos [−1] pos [1] pos [−2]

the set containing the top z IG values. Then, for each example in T whose value for A is not in SV, we replace that value by a common dummy value. Observe that z is a parameter of the ETL algorithm.

Note that this preprocessing is used only at the DT learning stage. All feature values are maintained at the transformation rule learning stage.

2.4 Template Evolution

TBL training time is highly sensitive to the number and complexity of the applied templates. Curran and Wong [6] argued that we can better tune the *training time* versus *templates complexity* trade-off by using an evolutionary template approach. The main idea is to apply only a small number of templates that evolve throughout the training. When training starts, templates are short, consisting of few feature combinations. As training proceeds, templates evolve to more complex ones that contain more feature combinations. In this way, only a few templates are considered at any point in time. Nevertheless, the descriptive power is not significantly reduced.

ETL provides an easy scheme to implement the template evolution strategy. First, we partition the learned template set by template size. Let T_k be the template set containing all templates of size k, where $k = 1, ..., K$ and K equals to the largest template size. Next, we split the TBL step into K consecutive phases. In phase k, TBL learns rules using only templates from T_k. For instance, using the tree shown in Fig. 2.4, we have four TBL training phases. In Table 2.1, we show the template sets used in the four TBL phases when the tree shown in Fig. 2.4 is used.

Using the template evolution strategy, the training time is decreased by a factor of five for the English phrase chunking task. This is a remarkable reduction, since we use an implementation of the *fastTBL* algorithm [25] that is already a very fast TBL version. Training time is a very important issue when modeling a system with a corpus-based approach. A fast ML strategy enables the testing of different modeling options, such as different feature sets. The efficacy of the rules generated by ETL template evolution is quite similar to the one obtained by training with all the templates at the sametime.

2.5 Template Sampling

Although the template evolution strategy produces a significant speedup in the ETL training time, it has a poor performance when it is necessary to learn all the possible rules at each consecutive TBL phase. If an excessive number of rules are learned in the earlier phases, the posterior phases will have just a few errors to correct. However, the main problem is that the templates of the earlier phases are very simple and may generate poor rules if all the rules with positive score are learned. Therefore, in cases where it is necessary to learn the largest rule set possible, template evolution is not suitable. On the other hand, in many cases this is not a problem. Usually, in order to avoid overfitting, we only learn rules whose score is at least two.

Nevertheless, there are cases where the learning of the largest rule set is necessary. For instance, when training an ensemble of classifiers using different training data sets, overfitting can be beneficial. This is because, in this specific case, overfitting can introduce diversity among the ensemble members. As an example, some DT ensemble learning methods do not use pruning [1, 2, 17].

In our ETL implementation, we also include the *template sampling* functionality, which consists in training the ETL model using only a randomly chosen fraction of the generated templates. Besides being simple, this strategy provides a speed up control that is very useful when multiple ETL models are to be learned.

2.6 Redundant Transformation Rules

As previously noticed by Florian [13], the TBL learning strategy shows a total lack of redundancy in modeling the training data. Only the rule that corrects the largest number of errors is selected at each learning iteration. All alternative rules that may correct the same errors, or a subset of the errors, are ignored. This greedy behavior is not a problem when the feature values tested in the alternative rules and the ones tested in the selected rule always co-occur. Unfortunately, this is not always the case when dealing with sparse data.

Florian includes redundancy in his TBL implementation by adding to the list of rules, after the training phase has completed, all the rules that do not introduce error. Florian shows that these additional rules improve the TBL performance for tasks were a word classification is independent of the surrounding word classifications.

In our ETL implementation, we also include redundancy in the TBL step, but in a different way. At each iteration, when the best rule b is learned, the algorithm also learns all the rules that do not include errors and correct exactly the same examples corrected by b. These redundant rules do not alter the error-driven learning strategy, since they do not provide any change in the training data. Their inclusion is compatible with the standard TBL framework, in the sense that applying the resulting rule set for the training data results in the same number of errors, with or without redundant rules. This kind of redundancy is more effective for low scored rules, since they are more likely to use sparse feature values and their selection is supported by just a few examples.

For the four tasks presented in this work, the inclusion of redundant rules does not improve the performance of single ETL classifiers. Actually, in some cases there is a decrease in the classification performance. We believe this performance degradation is due to a greater overfitting. Redundant rules increase the overfitting because more information from the training set is included in the learned model. However, the inclusion of redundancy improves the classification quality when several classifiers are combined. Since overfitting can be beneficial when multiple classifiers are used.

2.7 Related Work

Liu et al. [20] present a method for automatic template generation that uses DT. In their method, the tree-guided transformation-based learning (TTBL), two DT's are generated: one that uses all the examples and another that uses only the examples wrongly classified by the initial classifier. They produce the template set by extracting templates from the two trees. They use the second tree with the aim of producing templates that focus on the errors in the initial classification. Liu et al. apply the TTBL strategy to eliminate homograph ambiguity in a Mandarin text-to-speech system. For this task, TTBL obtains results comparable to the ones of handcrafted templates. TTBL is similar to ETL in the sense that they extract templates from DTs. However, the ETL template generation process is more versatile, since it uses the initial classification as an input feature. The ETL *true class trick* enables the use of the current classification feature in an effective way. Moreover, ETL [8] has been published earlier than TTBL [20].

An evolutionary scheme based on genetic algorithms (GA) to automatically generate TBL templates is presented by Milidiú et al. [21, 22]. Using a simple genetic coding, the generated template sets show an efficacy close to the one of handcrafted templates. The main drawback of this strategy is that the GA step is computationally expensive, since it is necessary to run the TBL algorithm in order to compute the fitness for each individual of the population. If we need to consider a large context window or a large number of features, it becomes infeasible.

Corston-Oliver and Gamon [5] present a combination of DTs and TBL. They derive candidate rules from the DT, and use TBL to select and apply them. Their work is restricted to binary features only. ETL strategy extracts more general knowledge from the DT, since it builds rule templates. Furthermore, ETL is applied to any kind of discrete features.

Carberry et al. [4] introduce a randomized version of the TBL framework. For each error, they try just a few randomly chosen templates from the given template set. This strategy speeds up the TBL training process, enabling the use of large template sets. However, they use handcrafted templates and variations of them, which implies that a template designer is still necessary.

Hwang et al [18] use DT decomposition to extract complex feature combinations for the weighted probabilistic sum model (WPSM). They also extract feature combinations that use only some nodes in a tree path. This is required to improve the effectiveness of the WPSM learning. Their work is similar to ours, since they use DT's for feature extraction. Nevertheless, the ETL learned template set is simpler than theirs, and is enough for effective TBL learning.

References

1. Banfield, R.E., Hall, L.O., Bowyer, K.W., Kegelmeyer, W.P.: Ensemble diversity measures and their application to thinning. Inf. Fusion **6**(1), 49–62 (2005)
2. Breiman, L.: Random forests. Mach. Learn. **45**(1), 5–32 (2001). doi:10.1023/A: 1010933404324
3. Brill, E.: Transformation-based error-driven learning and natural language processing: a case study in part-of-speech tagging. Comput. Linguist. **21**(4), 543–565 (1995)
4. Carberry, S., Vijay-Shanker, K., Wilson, A., Samuel, K.: Randomized rule selection in transformation-based learning: a comparative study. Nat. Lang. Eng. **7**(2), 99–116 (2001). doi:10.1017/S1351324901002662
5. Corston-Oliver, S., Gamon, M.: Combining decision trees and transformation-based learning to correct transferred linguistic representations. In: Proceedings of the Ninth Machine Tranlsation Summit, pp. 55–62. Association for Machine Translation in the Americas, New Orleans (2003)
6. Curran, J.R., Wong, R.K.: Formalisation of transformation-based learning. In: Proceedings of the ACSC, pp. 51–57, Canberra (2000)
7. Dash, M., Liu, H.: Feature selection for classification. Intell. Data Anal. **1**, 131–156 (1997)
8. dos Santos, C.N., Milidiú, R.L.: Entropy guided transformation learning. Technical Report 29/07, Departamento de Informática, PUC-Rio (2007). http://bib-di.inf.puc-rio.br/techreports/2007.htm
9. dos Santos, C.N., Milidiú, R.L.: Probabilistic classifications with TBL. In: Proceedings of Eighth International Conference on Intelligent Text Processing and Computational Linguistics—CICLing, pp. 196–207, Mexico (2007)
10. dos Santos, C.N., Oliveira, C.: Constrained atomic term: widening the reach of rule templates in transformation based learning. In: Portuguese Conference on Artificial Intelligence—EPIA, pp. 622–633 (2005)
11. Elming, J.: Transformation-based corrections of rule-based MT. In: Proceedings of the EAMT 11th Annual Conference, Oslo (2006)
12. Florian, R.: Named entity recognition as a house of cards: classifier stacking. In: Proceedings of CoNLL-2002, pp. 175–178, Taipei (2002)
13. Florian, R.: Transformation based learning and data-driven lexical disambiguation: syntactic and semantic ambiguity resolution. Ph.D. Thesis, The Johns Hopkins University (2002)
14. Florian, R., Henderson, J.C., Ngai, G.: Coaxing confidences from an old friend: probabilistic classifications from transformation rule lists. In: Proceedings of Joint Sigdat Conference on Empirical Methods in NLP and Very Large Corpora. Hong Kong University of Science and Technology, Kowloon (2000)
15. Forman, G., Guyon, I., Elisseeff, A.: An extensive empirical study of feature selection metrics for text classification. J. Mach. Learn. Res. **3**, 1289–1305 (2003)
16. Higgins, D.: A transformation-based approach to argument labeling. In: Ng, H.T., Riloff, E. (eds.) HLT-NAACL 2004 Workshop: Eighth Conference on Computational Natural Language Learning (CoNLL-2004), pp. 114–117. Association for Computational Linguistics, Boston (2004)

17. Ho, T.K.: The random subspace method for constructing decision forests. IEEE Trans. Pattern Anal. Mach. Intell. **20**(8), 832–844 (1998). doi:10.1109/34.709601
18. Hwang, Y.S., Chung, H.J., Rim, H.C.: Weighted probabilistic sum model based on decision tree decomposition for text chunking. Int. J. Comput. Process. Orient. Lang. **16**(1), 1–20 (2003)
19. Kudo, T., Matsumoto, Y.: Chunking with support vector machines. In: Proceedings of the NAACL-2001 (2001)
20. Liu, F., Shi, Q., Tao, J.: Tree-guided transformation-based homograph disambiguation in mandarin TTS system. In: IEEE International Conference on Acoustics, Speech and Signal Processing (ICASSP), pp. 4657–4660, Cambridge (2008)
21. Milidiú, R.L., Duarte, J.C., dos Santos, C.N.: Evolutionary TBL template generation. J. Braz. Comput. Soc. **13**(4), 39–50 (2007)
22. Milidiú, R.L., Duarte, J.C., dos Santos, C.N.: TBL template selection: an evolutionary approach. In: Proceedings of Conference of the Spanish Association for Artificial Intelligence—CAEPIA, Salamanca (2007)
23. Milidiú, R.L., dos Santos, C.N., Duarte, J.C.: Phrase chunking using entropy guided transformation learning. In: Proceedings of the 46th Annual Meeting of the Association for Computational Linguistics: Human Language Technologies—ACL-08: HLT, Columbus (2008)
24. Mitchell, T.M.: Machine Learning. McGraw-Hill, New York (1997)
25. Ngai, G., Florian, R.: Transformation-based learning in the fast lane. In: Proceedings of North Americal ACL, pp. 40–47 (2001)
26. Quinlan, J.R.: Induction of decision trees. Mach. Learn. **1**(1), 81–106 (1986). doi:10.1023/A: 1022643204877
27. Quinlan, J.R.: C4.5: programs for machine learning. Morgan Kaufmann, San Francisco (1993)
28. Ramshaw, L., Marcus, M.: Exploring the statistical derivation of transformational rule sequences for part-of-speech tagging. In: Proceedings of the Balancing Act-Workshop on Combining Symbolic and Statistical Approaches to Language, pp. 86–95. Association for Computational Linguistics, Toulouse (1994). http://www.citeseer.ist.psu.edu/article/ramshaw94exploring.html
29. Ramshaw, L., Marcus, M.: Text chunking using transformation-based learning. In: Armstrong, S., Church, K., Isabelle, P., Manzi, S., Tzoukermann, E., Yarowsky, D. (eds.) Natural Language Processing Using Very Large Corpora. Kluwer, Dordrecht (1999)
30. Su, J., Zhang, H.: A fast decision tree learning algorithm. In: Proceedings of the Twenty-First National Conference on Artificial Intelligence—AAAI (2006)
31. Surdeanu, M., Johansson, R., Meyers, A., Màrquez, L., Nivre, J.: The CoNLL 2008 shared task on joint parsing of syntactic and semantic dependencies. In: CoNLL 2008: Proceedings of the Twelfth Conference on Computational Natural Language Learning, pp. 159–177. Coling 2008 Organizing Committee, Manchester (2008). http://www.aclweb.org/anthology/W08-2121

Chapter 3
ETL Committee

Abstract In this chapter, we present ETL committee, an ensemble method that uses ETL as a base learner. The ETL committee strategy relies on the use of training data manipulation to create an ensemble of ETL classifiers. ETL committee combines the main ideas of bagging and random subspaces. From bagging, we borrow the bootstrap sampling method. From random subspaces, we use the feature sampling idea. In the ETL committee training, we use ETL with template sampling, which provides an additional randomization step. As far as we know, this is the first study that uses transformation rule learning as the base learner for an ensemble method. This chapter is organized as follows. In Sect. 3.1, we explain the main idea behind ensemble methods. In Sect. 3.2, we detail the ETL committee training phase. In Sect. 3.3, we detail the classification phase. Finally, in Sect. 3.4, we present some related works.

Keywords Machine learning · Ensemble methods · Entropy guided transformation learning · Decision trees · ETL committee · Bagging · Random subspaces · Random forests · Bootstrap sampling

3.1 Ensemble Algorithms

The combination of multiple classifiers is a general machine learning approach [4, 5, 7–9, 11]. Ensemble methods are learning algorithms that generate multiple individual classifiers and combine them to classify new samples. Usually, the final classification is done by taking a weighted or majority vote of the individual predictions. Such combinations of models are known as *ensemble models* or *committees*. The main purpose of model combination is to reduce the generalization error of a classifier. The *generalization error* is the error that a classifier makes on data not used in the training stage. Ensemble algorithms have received considerable attention in the last years [2, 3, 6, 10, 12, 13].

C. N. dos Santos and R. L. Milidiú, *Entropy Guided Transformation Learning*: *Algorithms and Applications*, SpringerBriefs in Computer Science, DOI: 10.1007/978-1-4471-2978-3_3, © The Author(s) 2012

According to Dietterich [7], a necessary and sufficient condition for an ensemble of classifiers to have a lower generalization error than any of its individual members is that the classifiers are accurate and diverse. A classifier is considered to be accurate if its error rate on new data is lower than just guessing. Two classifiers are diverse if they make different errors on new data. Several methods have been suggested for the creation of ensemble of classifiers [7]. Most ensemble methods differ on how they create diversity among the committee members. The manipulation of the training examples is commonly used to provide diverse classifiers [4, 5, 11].

Some general ensemble modeling strategies are bootstrap aggregating (bagging), random subspaces and boosting. The *bagging* method, introduced by Breiman [4], creates an ensemble of classifiers by making multiple replicates of the training set and using these as new training sets. These replicates are created using bootstrap sampling, which is the process of sampling at random with replacement from a data set. The *random subspaces* method, introduced by Ho [11], generates different classifiers by using different randomly chosen feature subsets. The *Adaboost* algorithm, introduced by Freund and Schapire [9], sequentially creates classifiers using a training set with weighted examples. In the Adaboost learning process, examples that are incorrectly predicted by a classifier have their weights increased for the next iteration.

3.2 Training Phase

Given a labeled training set $\mathcal{T}$, the ETL committee algorithm generates l ETL classifiers using different versions of $\mathcal{T}$. In Fig. 3.1, we detail the ETL committee training phase. The creation of each classifier is independent from the others. Therefore, the committee training process can be easily parallelized. In the creation of a classifier c, the first step consists in using *bootstrap sampling* to produce a bootstrap replicate $\mathcal{T}'$ of the training set $\mathcal{T}$. Next, *feature sampling* is applied to $\mathcal{T}'$, generating the training set $\mathcal{T}''$. Finally, in the *ETL training* step, a rule set is learned using $\mathcal{T}''$ as a training set. These steps are detailed in the following subsections. In Appendix A, we show some experimental results that highlight the contribution of each one of these steps to the committee behavior.

3.2.1 Bootstrap Sampling

In the *bootstrap sampling* step, a new version of the training set is generated using bootstrapping. *Bootstrapping* consists of sampling at random with replacement from the training set to generate an artificial training set of the same size as the original one. Hence, given a training set $\mathcal{T}$ consisting of n examples, a bootstrap replicate $\mathcal{T}'$ is constructed by sampling n examples at random, with replacement, from $\mathcal{T}$. Bootstrapping is the central idea of the bagging ensemble method, where it is used to provide diversity among the ensemble members.

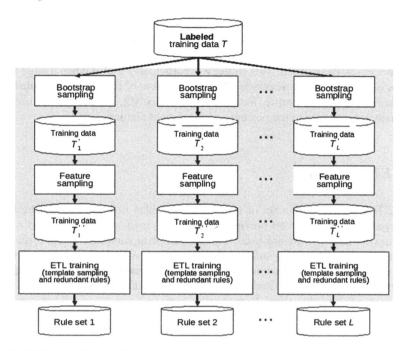

Fig. 3.1 ETL committee training phase

According to Breiman [4], an ensemble of classifiers trained on different bootstrap replicates can be effective if the base learner is *unstable*. An unstable classifier is one where small changes in the training set result in large changes in its predictions. Due to the greedy nature of the TBL learning process, rule selection is very sensitive to the occurrence of just a few examples. Usually, the rules in the tail of the learned rule set are selected based on just one or two error corrections. Therefore, we believe that small changes in the training set are able to significantly change the learned rule set. Moreover, since ETL uses DT to obtain templates and DT is an unstable learner [4], there is variability between the template sets generated from different bootstrap replicates. The use of different template sets has the potential to increase the ensemble diversity.

The number of bootstrap replicates is called the *ensemble size*. In Appendix A.1, we investigate the behavior of the ETL committee performance as the number of committee members increases.

3.2.2 Feature Sampling

In the *feature sampling* step, a new version of the training set is generated by randomly selecting a subset of the available features. The manipulation of the input feature set is a general technique for generating multiple classifiers. As each classifier is generated using a randomly drawn feature subset, the diversity among the ensemble members tends to increase. Feature sampling is the main idea used in the random subspaces ensemble method. This strategy is particularly useful when a large set of features is available. The percentage of input features to be included in the subset is a parameter of the ETL committee method. In Appendix A.2, we analyse the ensemble performance sensitivity to the percentage of sampled features.

3.2.3 ETL Training

In the *ETL training* step, a set of transformation rules is learned using the training set resulted from the two previous steps. Here, *template sampling* and *redundant transformation rules* are used. We use template sampling for two reasons: (1) it provides more diversity among the ensemble members, since it increases the chance of each classifier to be trained with a very different template set; (2) it speeds up the training process, since less templates are used, enabling the learning of larger rule sets in a reasonable time. Note that by sampling templates we are sampling feature combinations. Hence, the template sampling can be seen as a kind of feature sampling at the base learner level. The number of templates to be sampled is a parameter of the ETL committee method.

We use redundant rules since it increases the overfitting, and more information from the training set is included in the learned model. Overfitting is another way to introduce diversity among the ensemble members. For instance, DT's are usually not pruned when used as a base learner [1, 5, 11]. We use redundant rules in all ETL committee experiments reported in this book. In Appendix A.3, we analyse the contribution of redundant rules for the ETL committee performance.

3.3 Classification Phase

In Fig. 3.2, we detail the ETL committee classification phase. When classifying new data, each rule set is independently applied to the input data. For each data point, each ETL model gives a classification, and we say the model "votes" for that class. The final data point classification is computed by majority voting.

A drawback of our proposed ETL committee, as well as the other ensemble methods, is that it increases the classification time. For instance, when using an ensemble of size 100, the classification time is 100 times slower than the one of a single ETL classifier. However, this process can be easily parallelized, since the application of each rule set is independent from the others.

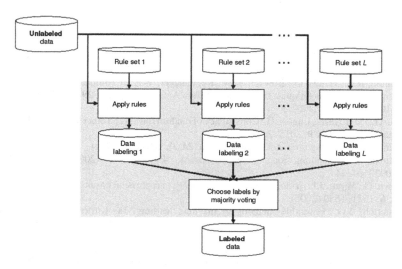

Fig. 3.2 ETL committee classification phase

3.4 Related Work

Breiman [5] presents an ensemble model called *Random Forest*, which uses boot-strapping and feature sampling. In the Random Forest Learning process, first, bootstrap sampling is employed to generate multiple replicates of the training set. Then, a decision tree is grown for each training set replicate. When growing a tree, a subset of the available features is randomly selected at each node, the best split available within those features is selected for that node. Each tree is grown to the largest extent possible, and there is no pruning. Random Forest is specific for decision trees, since the feature sampling step occurs at the base learner level. ETL committee differs from random forest in three main aspects: the base learner, where ETL is used; the feature sampling, which is done outside of the base learner; and the template sampling, which is a feature combination sampling method employed at the base learner level.

Panov and Dzeroski [13] describe an ensemble method that also combines bagging and random subspaces. Their intention is to achieve an algorithm whose behaviour is similar to the one of random forests, but with the advantage of being applicable to any base learner. Their method uses bootstrap sampling followed by feature sampling to generate different training sets. They show that, when using DT as a base learner, their approach has a comparable performance to that of random forests. The ETL committee method is similar to the one of Panov and Dzeroski in terms of training set manipulation. On the other hand, ETL committee differs from the Panov and Dzeroski approach because it includes template sampling, which is a randomization at the base learner level.

References

1. Banfield, R.E., Hall, L.O., Bowyer, K.W., Kegelmeyer, W.P.: Ensemble diversity measures and their application to thinning. Inf. Fusion **6**(1), 49–62 (2005)
2. Banfield, R.E., Hall, L.O., Bowyer, K.W., Kegelmeyer, W.P.: A comparison of decision tree ensemble creation techniques. IEEE Trans. Pattern Anal. Mach. Intell. **29**(1), 173–180 (2007). doi:10.1109/TPAMI.2007.2
3. Biau, G., Devroye, L., Lugosi, G.: Consistency of random forests and other averaging classifiers. J. Mach. Learn. Res. **9**, 2015–2033 (2008)
4. Breiman, L.: Bagging predictors. Mach. Learn. **24**(2), 123–140 (1996)
5. Breiman, L.: Random forests. Mach. Learn. **45**(1), 5–32 (2001). doi:10.1023/A:1010933404324
6. Brown, G., Wyatt, J.L., Tiňo, P.: Managing diversity in regression ensembles. J. Mach. Learn. Res. **6**, 1621–1650 (2005)
7. Dietterich, T.G.: Ensemble methods in machine learning. In: Kittler, J., Roli, F. (eds.) MCS '00: Proceedings of the First International Workshop on Multiple Classifier Systems, pp. 1–15. Springer, London (2000)
8. Florian, R., Ittycheriah, A., Jing, H., Zhang, T.: Named entity recognition through classifier combination. In: Daelemans, W., Osborne, M. (eds.) Proceedings of CoNLL-2003, pp. 168–171. Edmonton, Canada (2003)
9. Freund, Y., Schapire, R.E.: A decision-theoretic generalization of on-line learning and an application to boosting. J. Comput. Syst. Sci. **55**(1), 119–139 (1997)
10. García-Pedrajas, N., Ortiz-Boyer, D.: Boosting random subspace method. Neural Netw. **21**(9), 1344–1362 (2008). doi:10.1016/j.neunet.2007.12.046
11. Ho, T.K.: The random subspace method for constructing decision forests. IEEE Trans. Pattern Anal. Mach. Intell. **20**(8), 832–844 (1998). doi:10.1109/34.709601
12. Oza, N.C., Tumer, K.: Classifier ensembles: select real-world applications. Inf. Fusion **9**(1), 4–20 (2008). doi:10.1016/j.inffus.2007.07.002
13. Panov, P., Dzeroski, S.: Combining bagging and random subspaces to create better ensembles. In: Berthold, M.R., ShaweTaylor, J., Lavrac, N. (eds.) 7th International Symposium on Intelligent Data Analysis, pp. 118–129. Ljubljana, Slovenia (2007)

Part II
Entropy Guided Transformation
Learing: Applications

Chapter 4
General ETL Modeling for NLP Tasks

Abstract In this chapter we present some general entropy guided transformation learning configurations used for natural language processing tasks. We use the same configuration when applying ETL for the four examined tasks. Hence, the ETL modeling phase is performed with little effort. Moreover, the use of a common parameter setting can also provide some insight about the robustness of the learning algorithm. This chapter is organized as follows. In Sect. 4.1, we show how to model NLP tasks as classification tasks. In Sect. 4.2, we present the basic ETL parameter setting. In Sect. 4.3, we present the ETL committee parameter setting. In Sect. 4.4, we detail the performance measures used to assess the system performances on NLP tasks. Finally, in Sect. 4.5, we describe the software and hardware used in our experiments.

Keywords Machine learning · Natural language processing · Classification · Entropy guided transformation learning · Decision trees · ETL committee

4.1 Modeling

Although transformation rules can be used in more general processing tasks, ETL is concerned only with classification tasks. Hence, the problems for which ETL is applied must be cast as classification tasks. Fortunately, most NLP tasks are easily modeled this way.

In this work, the four examined tasks are modeled as token classification problems. Which means that, given a text, the learned system must predict a class label for each text token. Here, a *token* is a word or a punctuation mark. Each token provides an *example*, which corresponds to the list of feature values in the local context of the token. The local context of a token comprises the token itself and the adjacent ones. The number of tokens in the context defines the size of what is called the *context window*. For instance, using a size three context window, the following sentence

C. N. dos Santos and R. L. Milidiú, *Entropy Guided Transformation Learning:*
Algorithms and Applications, SpringerBriefs in Computer Science,
DOI: 10.1007/978-1-4471-2978-3_4, © The Author(s) 2012

Table 4.1 Examples derived from a sequence of tokens

ID	word[-1]	pos[-1]	word[0]	pos[0]	word[1]	pos[1]
1	EOS	EOS	The	DT	carriers	NNS
2	The	DT	carriers	NNS	were	VBD
3	carriers	NNS	were	VBD	competing	VBG
4	were	VBD	competing	VBG	fiercely	RB
5	competing	VBG	fiercely	RB	for	IN
6	fiercely	RB	for	IN	market	NN
7	for	IN	market	NN	share	NN
8	market	NN	share	NN	.	.
9	share	NN	.	.	EOS	EOS

produces the nine examples shown in Table 4.1. In this case, each token contains the features *word* and *POS tag*. Here, EOS tag indicates the start or end of a sentence.

```
The/DT carriers/NNS were/VBD competing/VBG
fiercely/RB for/IN market/NN share/NN ./.
```

4.2 Basic Parameter Setting

In all experiments presented in this work, we configure ETL as described below. The parameters are empirically tuned using the training and development sets available for the NER and SRL tasks. We also perform a 10-fold cross-validation using the SNR-CLIC Corpus, a Portuguese PCK corpus that is described in Sect. 6.1. We choose the common parameter setting that provides the best results for these three tasks.

We use this common parameter setting in our experiments with all tasks. This is recommended to verify the robustness of the ETL approach. Next, we list the setup.

Context window: we use a context window of size 7, which is the usual size for the four tasks.

Template size: we use templates which combine at most six features. Therefore, when extracting templates from DTs, the extraction process examines only the six first DT levels.

High dimensional features: we use the high dimensional feature preprocessing step for the feature *word*. We set the z parameter to 200.

Rule score threshold: we let the ETL algorithm learn rules whose score is at least two.

We report results for ETL trained with all the templates at the same time as well as using template evolution. In the template evolution all the parameters are maintained.

4.3 Committee Parameter Setting

In all experiments presented in this work, we configure ETL committee as described below. We use a common parameter setting in order to simplify our experiments, as well as to verify the robustness of ETL committee.

Bootstrap sampling: we use sentences as sampling units for bootstrapping. We set the ensemble size to 100. For all tested data sets, using more than 100 classifiers does not improve significantly the ensemble performance.

Feature sampling: we use 0.9 as the default value for the feature sampling para-meter. Which means that we randomly choose 90% of the available features when creating each model. Using a greater sampling rate may degrade the results for tasks which have a few number of features. However, we observe that this para-meter can be specifically tuned to improve the committee performance for a given training set.

ETL training: we train the ETL model to learn the largest rule set possible. We use 50 as the default number of templates to be sampled in the creation of each classifier. Using this amount of templates provides a reasonable training time speedup. However, we use 100 templates for SRL. This is because SRL involves a large number of features, which produces a larger number of templates. For instance, almost 650 templates are generated for the SRL task, while about 100 templates are generated for the PCK task.

4.4 Performance Measures

When performing token classification, the *token-by-token accuracy* is the usual sys-tem performance measure. The token-by-token accuracy is formalized by the fol-lowing equation.

$$Accuracy = \frac{\text{\# of correctly classified tokens}}{\text{\# of tokens in the test set}} \tag{4.1}$$

Precision, recall and F-measure are performance measures usually applied for information extraction tasks such as PCK, NER and SRL. *Precision* informs how many correct items the system extracted amongst all extracted items. *Recall* informs how many correct items the system extracted amongst all existing items. *F-measure* is the weighted harmonic mean of precision and recall. As usual, we use the $F_{\beta=1}$-measure, where recall and precision are evenly weighted. The following equations formalize precision, recall and $F_{\beta=1}$.

$$Precision = \frac{\text{\# of correctly extracted items}}{\text{\# of extracted items}} \tag{4.2}$$

$$Recall = \frac{\# \ of \ correctly \ extracted \ items}{\# \ of \ items \ in \ the \ test \ set} \tag{4.3}$$

$$F_{\beta=1} = \frac{2 * Precision * Recall}{Precision + Recall} \tag{4.4}$$

We also use the $F_{\beta=1} error$, which is given by the following equation.

$$F_{\beta=1} error = 100 - F_{\beta=1} \tag{4.5}$$

4.5 Software and Hardware

Our current ETL implementation uses the C4.5 system [2] to learn decision trees. In order to learn transformation rules, we have implemented the fastTBL algorithm [1] using the Python programming language.

The ETL experiments are performed using an Intel® Centrino® Duo 1.66 GHz notebook with 2 GB of RAM memory.

The ETL committee experiments are performed using a cluster of 15 machines. Each machine has 2 GB of RAM memory and an Intel® Pentium® D CPU 3.40 GHz with 2 cores. Therefore, the cluster has 30 CPU cores. Since the training of each classifier is independent from the others, the ETL committee experiments are easily parallelized. When training a committee, we run the same code in the 30 different cores.

References

1. Ngai, G., Florian, R.: Transformation-based learning in the fast lane. In: Proceedings of North Americal ACL, pp. 40–47 (2001)
2. Quinlan, J.R.: C4.5: programs for machine learning. Morgan Kaufmann Publishers Inc., San Francisco (1993)

Chapter 5
Part-of-Speech Tagging

Abstract This chapter presents the application of ETL to language independent part-of-speech (POS) tagging. The POS tagging task consists in assigning a POS or another lexical class marker to each word in a text. We apply ETL and ETL Committee to four different corpora in three different languages: Portuguese, German and English. ETL system achieves state-of-the-art results for the four corpora. The ETL Committee strategy slightly improves the ETL accuracy for all corpora. This chapter is organized as follows. In Sect. 5.1, we describe the task and the selected corpora. In Sect. 5.2, we detail some modeling configurations used in our POS tagger system. In Sect. 5.3, we show some configurations used in the machine learning algorithms. Section 5.4 presents the application of ETL for the Mac-Morpho Corpus. In Sect. 5.5, we describe the application of ETL for the Tycho Brahe Corpus. Section 5.6 presents the application of ETL for the TIGER Corpus. In Sect. 5.7, we show the application of ETL for the Brown Corpus. Finally, Sect. 5.8 presents some concluding remarks.

Keywords Machine learning · Natural language processing · Part-of-speech tagging · Entropy guided transformation learning · ETL committee · Transformation based learning

5.1 Task and Corpora

Part-of-speech tagging is the process of assigning a POS or another lexical class marker to each word in a text [8]. POS tags classify words into categories, based on the role they play in the context in which they appear. The POS tag is a key input feature for NLP tasks like phrase chunking and named entity recognition. In the example that follows, which was extrated from the Mac-Morpho Corpus, the POS tags have the following meanings: N = *noun*, ADJ = *adjective*, KC = *coordinating conjunction*, PREP = *preposition*, and V = *verb*.

C. N. dos Santos and R. L. Milidiú, *Entropy Guided Transformation Learning:*
Algorithms and Applications, SpringerBriefs in Computer Science,
DOI: 10.1007/978-1-4471-2978-3_5, © The Author(s) 2012

Table 5.1 Part-of-speech tagging corpora

Corpus	Language	Tagset size	Training data		Test data	
			Sent.	Tokens	Sent.	Tokens
Mac-Morpho	Portuguese	22	44,233	1,007,671	9,141	213,794
Tycho Brahe	Portuguese	383	30,698	775,601	10,234	259,991
TIGER	German	54	41,954	742,189	8,520	146,389
Brown	English	182	47,027	950,975	10,313	210,217

```
Safra/N recorde/ADJ e/KC disponibilidade/N de/PREP
   crédito/N ativam/V vendas/N de/PREP máquinas/N
              agrícolas /ADJ ./.
```

We apply ETL to four different POS tagged corpora in three different languages. The selected corpora are: Mac-Morpho [1], a Portuguese language corpus; Tycho Brahe [7], a Portuguese language corpus; TIGER [2], a German language corpus; and Brown [6], an English language corpus. In Table 5.1, we show some characteristics of these corpora.

The Mac-Morpho Corpus is tagged with 22 POS tags, while the Tycho Brahe Corpus is tagged with 383 POS tags. The TIGER Corpus is tagged with 54 POS tags, and the Brown Corpus is tagged with 182 POS tags. Both the Tycho Brahe Corpus and the Brown Corpus use more POS tags because these tags also identify morphological aspects such as word number and gender. Each corpus is divided into training and test sets. For the Portuguese corpora, these training and test set splits are the same as reported by Milidiú et al. [9].

5.2 POS Tagging Modeling

In POS tagging, a word is called a *known word* if it appears in the training set. Otherwise, it is called an *unknown word*. Usually, POS tagging systems handle unknown words in a separate way. Brill [4] proposes a POS tagging modeling for TBL that consists of two stages: the *morphological*, which classifies the unknown words using morphological information; and the *contextual*, which classifies the known and unknown words using contextual information. Our POS tagging modeling approach follows the two stages strategy proposed by Brill. The following sections detail the two stages.

5.2.1 Morphological Stage

In the morphological stage, *morphological rules* are used to classify the unknown words. TBL is used to learn the morphological rules. These rules are based on the following token features:

- up to c characters long word prefixes and suffixes;
- specific character occurrence in a word;
- adding (or subtracting) a c characters long prefix (or suffix) results in a known word;
- occurrence of the word before (or after) a specific word W in a given long list of word bigrams. For instance, if the word appears after "to", then it is likely to be a verb in the infinitive form.

In our experiments, we set the parameter c equal to 5.

With a very simple template set [4], one can effectively perform the morphological stage. For this stage, it is enough to use one feature or two feature templates of the token been classified. The one feature templates use one of the current token features. The two feature templates use one of the current token features and the current token POS. We do not use ETL to train the morphological stage, since the templates used here are very simple. Therefore, in our experiments, the TBL-based morphological stage is part of the baseline system.

5.2.2 Contextual Stage

In the contextual stage, contextual rules are used to correct errors in the classification of known and unknown words. The contextual rules use the features *word* and *POS* of any token in the defined context window. We use ETL for learning contextual rules only.

5.3 Machine Learning Modeling

We use the following task specific configurations.

BLS: the baseline system assigns to each word the POS tag that is most frequently associated with that word in the training set. Words that do not appear in the training set are classified by the morphological rules.

TBL: the results for the TBL approach refer to the contextual stage trained using the lexicalized template set proposed by Brill [4]. This template set uses combinations of *words* and *POS* in a context window of size seven.

ETL: in the ETL learning, we use the features *word* and *POS*. The default ETL parametrization shown in Chap. 4 is used.

ETL$_{TE}$: we use the same ETL configuration, but here we perform template evolution.

ETL$_{CMT}$: we use the default ETL committee parametrization shown in Sect. 4.3.

We also report the state-of-the-art system performance for each corpus.

Table 5.2 System performances for the Mac-Morpho Corpus

System	Accuracy (%)	# Templates
ETL$_{CMT}$	**96.94**	50
ETL	96.75	72
ETL$_{TE}$	96.74	72
TBL	96.60	26
BLS	91.66	–

5.4 Mac-Morpho Corpus

Santos et al. [5] present a TBL system with state-of-the-art performance for the Mac-Morpho Corpus. Therefore, for this corpus, we only report the performance of ETL, TBL and BLS systems.

In Table 5.2, we summarize the system performance results. The ETL system reduces the BLS accuracy error by 61%, from 8.34 to 3.25. ETL and TBL systems achieve similar accuracy. The ETL$_{TE}$ system reduces the ETL training time by 73%, from 214 to 58 min. This is a remarkable reduction, since we use an implementation of the *fastTBL* algorithm [10] that is already a very fast TBL version. Moreover, there is no accuracy reduction when using the template evolution approach. This suggests that, for this task, complex templates are not necessary for the earlier learned rules.

The ETL$_{CMT}$ system reduces the accuracy error by 6% when compared to the single ETL system. Its accuracy, 96.94%, is the best one reported so far for the Mac-Morpho Corpus. On the other hand, the classification with the ETL$_{CMT}$ system is 100 times slower than the one with the single ETL system.

5.5 Tycho Brahe Corpus

Santos et al. [5] present a TBL system with state-of-the-art performance for the Tycho Brahe Corpus. Therefore, for the Tycho Brahe Corpus, we only report the performance of ETL, TBL and BLS systems.

In Table 5.3, we summarize the system performance results. The ETL system reduces the BLS accuracy error by 52%, from 7.00 to 3.36. ETL and TBL systems achieve similar accuracy. The ETL$_{TE}$ system reduces the ETL training time by 65%, from 60 to 21 min. Moreover, there is no significant accuracy reduction when using the template evolution approach.

The ETL$_{CMT}$ system reduces the accuracy error by nearly 2.5% when compared to the single ETL system. The ETL$_{CMT}$ accuracy, 96.72%, is the best one reported so far for the Mac-Morpho Corpus.

Table 5.3 System
performances for the Tycho
Brahe Corpus

System	Accuracy (%)	# Templates
ETL$_{CMT}$	**96.72**	50
ETL	96.64	43
TBL	96.63	26
ETL$_{TE}$	96.60	43
BLS	93.00	–

Table 5.4 System
performances for the TIGER
Corpus

System	Accuracy (%)	# Templates
ETL$_{CMT}$	**96.68**	50
ETL$_{TE}$	96.58	66
ETL	96.57	66
TBL	96.53	26
BLS	93.31	–

5.6 TIGER Corpus

We have not found any work reporting the state-of-the-art performance for the TIGER Corpus. Therefore, for the TIGER Corpus, we report the performance of ETL, TBL and BLS systems.

In Table 5.4, we summarize the system performance results. The ETL system reduces the BLS accuracy error by 49%, from 6.69 to 3.43. ETL and TBL systems achieve similar accuracy. The ETL$_{TE}$ system reduces the ETL training time by 61%, from 57 to 22 min. Moreover, there is no accuracy reduction when using the template evolution approach. The ETL$_{CMT}$ system reduces the accuracy error by nearly 3% when compared to the single ETL system.

The TnT tagger [3], which is based on Hidden Markov Models, is a state-of-the-art system for German. It has been trained and tested on the NEGRA Corpus [11], which is the predecessor of the TIGER Corpus and uses the same tagset. For the NEGRA Corpus, Brants [3] reports an overall accuracy of 96.7%. Since both ETL and TBL systems performances for the TIGER Corpus are very close to the TnT performance for the NEGRA Corpus, we believe that both ETL and TBL systems achieve state-of-the-art performance for German POS tagging.

5.7 Brown Corpus

Eric Brill [4] presents a TBL system with state-of-the-art performance for the Brown Corpus. Therefore, for the Brown Corpus, we only report the performance of ETL, TBL and BLS systems.

In Table 5.5, we summarize the system performance results. The ETL system reduces the BLS accuracy error by 56%, from 7.57 to 3.31. ETL and TBL systems

Table 5.5 System performances for the Brown Corpus

System	Accuracy (%)	# Templates
ETL_{CMT}	**96.83**	50
ETL	96.69	63
TBL	96.67	26
ETL_{TE}	96.61	63
BLS	92.43	–

achieve similar accuracy. Therefore, ETL has state-of-the-art performance for the Brown Corpus. The ETL_{TE} system reduces the ETL training time by 68%, from 122 to 39 min. Moreover, there is no significant accuracy reduction when using the template evolution approach. The ETL_{CMT} system reduces the accuracy error by 4% when compared to the single ETL system.

5.8 Summary

This chapter presents the application of ETL to language independent POS tagging. We apply ETL to four different corpora in three different languages. The selected corpora are: Mac-Morpho, a Portuguese language corpus; Tycho Brahe, a Portuguese language corpus; TIGER, a German language corpus; and Brown, an English language corpus.

Using the default parameter setting and a common set of features, the ETL system achieves state-of-the-art results for the four corpora. ETL and TBL achieve similar results. This finding indicates that the entropy guided template generation employed by ETL is very effective for the POS tagging task. It is interesting to note that the template set handcrafted by Brill has shown to be very robust for language independent POS tagging. The TBL system trained with this template set achieves very good results for the four corpora. This suggests that the useful feature combinations for POS tagging of the three languages are very similar. This hypothesis can be confirmed when looking at the template sets generated by ETL, which share many templates. For instance, the template sets generated for Mac-Morpho and TIGER Corpus share 67% of the templates.

The rule application phase of ETL POS taggers is fast. For instance, our Python implementation of the ETL POS tagger created with the Mac-Morpho Corpus processes about 8,000 tokens per second.

The template evolution strategy provides a significant training time reduction in all cases. For the MAC-Morpho Corpus, the transformation learning is accelerated by a factor of almost four. Moreover, for all corpora, there is no significant accuracy reduction when using template evolution. This finding indicates that, for POS tagging, complex templates are not necessary for the earlier learned rules.

The ETL committee strategy slightly improves the ETL accuracy for all corpora. However, the result is more significant only for the Mac-Morpho Corpus, where an accuracy error reduction of 6% is achieved. Training a committee of 100 classifiers using the Mac-Morpho Corpus takes about 13 h on our 30 CPU-core cluster. While ETL committee is an interesting method to improve accuracy without additional human effort, its classification time is very expensive, since many classifiers are used. It may only be useful when a computer cluster is available.

These chapter results indicate that ETL and ETL committee are effective methods to produce competitive language independent POS taggers with little modeling effort.

References

1. Aluísio, S.M., Pelizzoni, J.M., Marchi, A.R., de Oliveira, L., Manenti, R., Marquiafável, V.: An account of the challenge of tagging a reference corpus for brazilian portuguese. In: Proceedings of the Workshop on Computational Processing of Written and Spoken Portuguese, pp. 110–117 (2003)
2. Brants, S., Dipper, S., Hansen, S., Lezius, W., Smith, G.: The TIGER treebank. In: Proceedings of the Workshop on Treebanks and Linguistic Theories, Sozopol (2002)
3. Brants, T.: Tnt—a statistical part-of-speech tagger. In: Proceedings of the Applied Natural Language Processing Conference, pp. 224–231 (2000)
4. Brill, E.: Transformation-based error-driven learning and natural language processing: a case study in part-of-speech tagging. Comput. Linguist. **21**(4), 543–565 (1995)
5. dos Santos, C.N., Milidiú, R.L., Rentería, R.P.: Portuguese part-of-speech tagging using entropy guided transformation learning. In: Proceedings of 8th Workshop on Computational Processing of Written and Spoken Portuguese, pp. 143–152. Aveiro, Portugal (2008)
6. Francis, W.N., Kucera, H.: Frequency analysis of english usage. Lexicon and grammar. Houghton Mifflin, Boston (1982)
7. IEL-UNICAMP, IME-USP: Corpus anotado do português histórico tycho brahe. http://www.ime.usp.br/~tycho/corpus/. Accessed 23 Jan 2008
8. Jurafsky, D., Martin, J.H.: Speech and Language Processing. Prentice Hall, New Jersey (2000)
9. Milidiú, R.L., dos Santos, C.N., Duarte, J.C.: Phrase chunking using entropy guided transformation learning. In: Proceedings of the 46th Annual Meeting of the Association for Computational Linguistics: Human Language Technologies—ACL-08: HLT. Columbus, Ohio (2008)
10. Ngai, G., Florian, R.: Transformation-based learning in the fast lane. In: Proceedings of North Americal ACL, pp. 40–47 (2001)
11. Skut, W., Krenn, B., Brants, T., Uszkoreit, H.: An annotation scheme for free word order languages. In: Proceedings of ANLP-97 (1997)

Chapter 6
Phrase Chunking

Abstract This chapter presents the application of ETL to language independent phrase chunking (PCK). The PCK task consists in dividing a text into non-overlapping phrases. We apply ETL and ETL committee to four different corpora in three different languages: Portuguese, English and Hindi. For the four corpora ETL system achieves very competitive results. For two copora ETL achieves state-of-the-art results. ETL committee significantly improves the ETL results for the four corpora. This chapter is organized as follows. In Sect. 6.1, we describe the task and the selected corpora. In Sect. 6.2, we detail some modeling configurations used in our PCK system. In Sect. 6.3, we show some configurations used in the machine learning algorithms. Section 6.4 presents the application of ETL for the SNR-CLIC Corpus. In Sect. 6.5, we detail the application of ETL for the Ramshaw and Marcus Corpus. Section 6.6 presents the application of ETL for the CoNLL-2000 Corpus. In Sect. 6.7, we present the application of ETL for the SPSAL-2007 Corpus. Finally, Sect. 6.8 presents some concluding remarks.

Keywords Machine learning · Natural language processing · Phrase chunking · Entropy guided transformation learning · ETL committee · Transformation based learning · Support vector machines · Conditional random fields · Hidden Markov models

6.1 Task and Corpora

Phrase chunking consists in dividing a text into non-overlapping phrases [7]. It provides a key feature that helps on more elaborated NLP tasks such as NER and SRL. In the example that follows, we use brackets to indicate the eight phrase chunks in the sentence. In this example, there are four Noun Phrases (NP), two Verb Phrases (VP) and two Prepositional Phrases (PP).

C. N. dos Santos and R. L. Milidiú, *Entropy Guided Transformation Learning: Algorithms and Applications*, SpringerBriefs in Computer Science, DOI: 10.1007/978-1-4471-2978-3_6, © The Author(s) 2012

Table 6.1 Phrase chunking corpora

Corpus	Language	Phrases	Training data		Test data	
			Sent.	Tokens	Sent.	Tokens
SNR-CLIC	Portuguese	NP	3,514	83,346	878	20,798
R&M	English	NP	8,936	211,727	2,012	47,377
CoNLL-2000	English	All	8,936	211,727	2,012	47,377
SPSAL-2007	Hindi	All	924	20,000	210	5,000

```
[NP He ] [VP reckons ] [NP the current account
  deficit] [VP will narrow] [PP to ] [NP only
    # 1.8 billion ] [PP in ] [NP September ]
```

We apply ETL to four different PCK corpora in three different languages. The selected corpora are: SNR-CLIC, a Portuguese NP chunking corpus [4]; Ramshaw and Marcus (R&M), an English base NP chunking corpus [6]; CoNLL-2000, an English phrase chunking corpus [7]; and SPSAL-2007, a Hindi phrase chunking corpus [2]. Table 6.1 shows some characteristics of these corpora.

The four corpora are annotated with *POS* and *PCK* tags. The *PCK tags* feature provides the phrase chunking annotation. For both corpora SNR-CLIC and Ramshaw and Marcus, the *PCK tags* feature uses the IOB1 tagging style, where: O, means that the word is not a phrase chunk; I, means that the word is part of a phrase chunk and B is used for the leftmost word of a phrase chunk beginning immediately after another phrase chunk. This tagging style is illustrated in the following noun phrase chunking example.

```
He/I  reckons/O  the/I  current/I  account/I  deficit/I will/O
narrow/O  to/O  only/I  #/I  1.8/I  billion/I in/O  September/I
```

For both corpora CoNLL-2000 and SPSAL-2007, the *PCK tags* feature uses the IOB2 tagging style, where: O, means that the word is not a phrase; B-X, means that the word is the first one of a phrase type X and I-X, means that the word is inside of a phrase type X. This tagging style is illustrated in the following phrase chunking example.

```
He/B-NP  reckons/B-VP  the/B-NP  current/I-NP  account/I-NP
deficit/I-NP will/B-VP narrow/I-VP  to/B-PP  only/B-NP  #/I-NP
    1.8/I-NP  billion/I-NP in/B-PP  September/B-NP
```

6.2 Phrase Chunking Modeling

When performing PCK, at both training and test time, we generate some *derived features*. This step is performed before the training and test time. It is described in the following section.

6.2.1 Derived Features

The training and test corpora provide three input features: *word*, *POS* and *PCK tags*. Using the input features, we produce the following two derived features:

- **Capitalization**: this feature classifies the words according to their capitalization. It assumes one of the following categorical values: First Letter is Uppercase, All Letters are Uppercase, All Letters are Lowercase, Number, Punctuation, Number with "/" or "-" inside or Other.
- **Left verb**: for each token, this feature assumes the word feature value of the nearest predecessor verb.

6.3 Machine Learning Modeling

We use the following task specific configurations.

BLS: the baseline system assigns to each word the *PCK tag* that was most frequently associated with the part-of-speech of that word in the training set. The only exception was the initial classification of prepositions in the SNR-CLIC Corpus. In this case, the initial classification is done on an individual basis: each preposition has its frequency individually measured and the NP tag is assigned accordingly, in a lexicalized method.

TBL: in the TBL system we use a template set proposed by Ramshaw and Marcus [6]. This set contains 100 handcrafted templates which make use of the features *word*, *POS* and *PCK tags* in a context window of size 7. For the SNR-CLIC Corpus we extend this template set by adding the set of six special templates proposed by Santos and Oliveira [3]. The Santos and Oliveira's six templates are designed to reduce classification errors of prepositions within the task of Portuguese noun phrase chunking. These templates use special handcrafted constraints that allow us to efficiently check the feature *word* in up to 20 left side adjacent tokens.

ETL: in the ETL learning, for the four corpora, we use the features *word*, *POS*, and *PCK tags*. The *left verb* feature is used only for the SNR-CLIC Corpus. The default ETL parameter setting shown in Sect. 4.2 is used. In order to make a fair comparison between ETL and TBL with handcrafted templates, we do not use the *capitalization* feature in the ETL system. Since this feature is not used in the Ramshaw and Marcus's template set.

ETL$_{TE}$: we use the same ETL configuration, but here we perform template evolution.

ETL$_{CMT}$: we use the default ETL committee parametrization shown in Sect. 4.3. Additionally we use the *capitalization* feature for the SNR-CLIC, Ramshaw and Marcus and CoNLL-2000 corpora.

We also report the state-of-the-art system performance for each corpus.

Table 6.2 System performances for the SNR-CLIC Corpus

System	Accuracy (%)	Precision (%)	Recall (%)	$F_{\beta=1}$	# Templates
ETL$_{CMT}$	**98.09**	**89.66**	**89.51**	**89.58**	50
ETL	97.97	88.77	88.93	88.85	46
ETL$_{TE}$	97.84	88.18	88.65	88.41	46
TBL	97.63	87.17	88.26	87.71	106
BLS	96.57	62.69	74.45	68.06	–

6.4 SNR-CLIC Corpus

Santos and Oliveira [3] present a TBL modeling that obtains state-of-the-art performance for Portuguese NP chunking. The TBL system presented in this section uses the same modeling presented by Santos and Oliveira. For the SNR-CLIC Corpus, we report the performance of ETL, TBL and BLS systems.

In Table 6.2, we summarize the system performance results. The ETL system reduces the BLS $F_{\beta=1}$ error by 65%, from 31.94 to 11.15. Here, the ETL system outperforms the TBL system by 1.14 in terms of $F_{\beta=1}$. The ETL$_{TE}$ system, which uses template evolution, has a training time 56% shorter than the one of ETL. However, there is a slightly performance loss in terms of $F_{\beta=1}$. The ETL$_{CMT}$ system reduces the $F_{\beta=1}$ error by 6.6% when compared to the single ETL system.

Observe that ETL generates only 46 template. However, this small template set is more effective than the handcrafted one, which has 106 templates. The number of templates generated by ETL is directly affected by the size of the training set. A small training set produces a small decision tree and, consequently, a small template set.

6.5 Ramshaw and Marcus Corpus

Kudo and Matsumoto [5] present an SVM-based system with state-of-the-art performance for the Ramshaw and Marcus Corpus. Therefore, for this corpus, we also list the SVM system performance reported by Kudo and Matsumoto.

In Table 6.3, we summarize the system performance results. The ETL system reduces the BLS $F_{\beta=1}$ error by 63%, from 20.01 to 7.41. ETL slightly outperforms TBL in terms of $F_{\beta=1}$. The ETL$_{TE}$ system reduces the ETL training time by 65%, from 21.31 to 7.43 min. Moreover, the template evolution strategy slightly increases the ETL $F_{\beta=1}$. This finding suggests that, for this corpus, complex templates are not necessary for the earlier learned rules.

The ETL$_{CMT}$ system reduces the $F_{\beta=1}$ error by 9.4% when compared to the single ETL system. The ETL$_{CMT}$ performance is competitive with the one of Kudo and Matsumoto's SVM system.

Table 6.3 System performances for the Ramshaw and Marcus Corpus

System	Accuracy (%)	Precision (%)	Recall (%)	$F_{\beta=1}$	# Templates
SVM	–	**94.15**	**94.29**	**94.22**	–
ETL$_{CMT}$	97.89	93.09	93.49	93.29	50
ETL$_{TE}$	97.61	92.56	93.04	92.80	106
ETL	97.52	92.49	92.70	92.59	106
TBL	97.42	91.68	92.26	91.97	100
BLS	94.48	78.20	81.87	79.99	–

Table 6.4 System performances for the CoNLL-2000 Corpus

System	Accuracy (%)	Precision (%)	Recall (%)	$F_{\beta=1}$	# Templates
SVM	–	**94.12**	**94.13**	**94.12**	–
ETL$_{CMT}$	95.85	93.11	93.42	93.27	50
ETL	95.13	92.24	92.32	92.28	183
ETL$_{TE}$	95.03	91.89	92.28	92.09	183
TBL	95.12	92.05	92.28	92.16	100
BLS	77.29	72.58	82.14	77.07	–

6.6 CoNLL-2000 Corpus

Wu et al. [8] present an SVM-based system with state-of-the-art performance for the CoNLL-2000 Corpus. Therefore, for this corpus, we also list the SVM system performance reported by Wu et al.

In Table 6.4, we summarize the system performance results. The ETL system reduces the BLS $F_{\beta=1}$ error by 66%, from 22.93 to 7.72. ETL, TBL and ETL$_{TE}$ systems have similar performance results. However, the ETL$_{TE}$ system reduces the ETL training time by 83%, from 160 to 30 min. The ETL$_{CMT}$ system significantly reduces the $F_{\beta=1}$ error by 13% when compared to the single ETL system. The ETL$_{CMT}$ performance is competitive with the one of the SVM system.

In Table 6.5, we show the ETL$_{CMT}$ system results, broken down by phrase chunk type, for the CoNLL-2000 Corpus.

6.7 SPSAL-2007 Corpus

Avinesh and karthick [1] present a state-of-the-art system for the Hindi SPSAL-2007 Corpus. Their system uses a combination of Hidden Markov models (HMM) and Conditional Random Fields (CRF). Therefore, for this corpus, we also list the HMM+CRF system performance reported by Avinesh and Karthick.

Table 6.5 ETL$_{CMT}$ results by chunk type for the CoNLL-2000 Corpus

Chunk Type	Precision (%)	Recall (%)	F$_{\beta=1}$
ADJP	80.46	72.37	76.20
ADVP	80.81	78.75	79.77
CONJP	38.46	55.56	45.45
INTJ	0.00	0.00	0.00
LST	0.00	0.00	0.00
NP	93.41	93.86	93.63
PP	96.49	98.38	97.43
PRT	72.22	73.58	72.90
SBAR	90.75	86.17	88.40
VP	92.95	93.34	93.14
Overall	93.11	93.42	93.27

Table 6.6 System performances for the SPSAL-2007 Corpus

System	Accuracy (%)	# Templates
HMM + CRF	**80.97**	–
ETL$_{CMT}$	80.44	50
ETL	78.53	30
TBL	78.53	100
ETL$_{TE}$	77.21	30
BLS	70.05	–

In Table 6.6, we summarize the system performance results. The results are reported in terms of chunking accuracy only, the same performance measure used in the SPSAL-2007 contest [2]. The ETL system reduces the BLS accuracy error by 28%, from 29.95 to 21.47. ETL and TBL systems achieve the same accuracy. The ETL$_{TE}$ system reduces the ETL training time by 50%. However, there is a decrease in the system accuracy. The ETL$_{CMT}$ system significantly reduces the accuracy error by 9% when compared to the single ETL system. The ETL$_{CMT}$ performance is similar to the one of the HMM+CRF system.

6.8 Summary

This chapter presents the application of ETL to language independent phrase chunking. We apply ETL to four different corpora in three different languages. The selected corpora are: SNR-CLIC, a Portuguese noun phrase chunking corpus; Ramshaw and Marcus, an English base noun phrase chunking corpus; CoNLL-2000, an English phrase chunking corpus; and SPSAL-2007, a Hindi phrase chunking corpus.

Using the default parameter setting and a common set of features, the ETL system achieves state-of-the-art results for two corpora: SNR-CLIC and SPSAL-

2007. For the other two, Ramshaw and Marcus and CoNLL-2000, the ETL system achieves state-of-the-art competitive results. ETL outperforms TBL with handcrafted templates in all the experiments. This finding indicates that the entropy guided template generation employed by ETL is very effective for the PCK task.

The rule application phase of ETL phrase chunkers is fast. For instance, our Python implementation of the ETL PCK created with the CoNLL-2000 Corpus processes about 12,000 tokens per second. The template evolution strategy provides a reasonable reduction of training time in all cases. For the CoNLL-2000 Corpus, the template evolution accelerates transformation learning by a factor of five. However, there is a slightly decrease in the ETL $F_{\beta=1}$.

ETL committee significantly improves the ETL results for the four corpora. For the CoNLL-2000 Corpus, ETL committee reduces the $F_{\beta=1}$ error by 13%, when compared to a single ETL model. Training a committee of 100 classifiers using the CoNLL-2000 Corpus takes about three and a half hours on our 30 CPU-core cluster.

These chapter results indicate that ETL and ETL committee are effective methods to produce competitive language independent PCK systems with little modeling effort.

References

1. Avinesh, P.V.S., Karthik, G.: Part-of-speech tagging and chunking using conditional random fields and transformation based learning. In: Proceedings of the IJCAI and the Workshop on Shallow Parsing for South Asian Languages, pp. 21–24 (2007)
2. Bharati, A., Mannem, P.R.: Introduction to shallow parsing contest on South Asian languages. In: Proceedings of the IJCAI and the Workshop On Shallow Parsing for South Asian Languages, pp. 1–8 (2007)
3. dos Santos, C.N., Oliveira, C.: Constrained atomic term: Widening the reach of rule templates in transformation based learning. In: Portuguese Conference on Artificial Intelligence—EPIA, pp. 622–633 (2005)
4. Freitas, M.C., Garrao, M., Oliveira, C., dos Santos, C.N., Silveira, M.: A anotação de um corpus para o aprendizado supervisionado de um modelo de sn. In: Proceedings of the III TIL / XXV Congresso da SBC. São Leopoldo (2005).
5. Kudo, T., Matsumoto, Y.: Chunking with support vector machines. In: Proceedings of the NAACL-2001 (2001)
6. Ramshaw, L., Marcus, M.: Text chunking using transformation-based learning. In: Yarovsky, D., Church, K. (eds.) Proceedings of the Third Workshop on Very Large Corpora, pp. 82–94. Association for Computational Linguistics, Somerset (1995)
7. Sang, E.F.T.K., Buchholz, S.: Introduction to the conll-2000 shared task: chunking. In: Proceedings of the 2nd Workshop on Learning Language in Logic and the 4th CONLL, pp. 127–132. Association for Computational Linguistics, Morristown (2000). doi:10.3115/1117601.1117631
8. Wu, Y.C., Chang, C.H., Lee, Y.S.: A general and multi-lingual phrase chunking model based on masking method. In: Proceedings of 7th International Conference on Intelligent Text Processing and Computational Linguistics, pp. 144–155 (2006)

Chapter 7
Named Entity Recognition

Abstract This chapter presents the application of ETL to language independent named entity recognition (NER). The NER task consists of finding all proper nouns in a text and classifying them among several given categories of interest. We apply ETL and ETL Committee to three different corpora in three different languages: Portuguese, Spanish and Dutch. ETL system achieves state-of-the-art competitive results for the three corpora. Moreover, ETL Committee significantly improves the ETL results for the three corpora. This chapter is organized as follows. In Sect. 7.1, we describe the NER task and the selected corpora. In Sect. 7.2, we detail some modeling configurations used in our NER system. In Sect. 7.3, we show some configurations used in the machine learning algorithms. Section 7.4 presents the application of ETL for the HAREM Corpus. In Sect. 7.5, we present the application of ETL for the SPA CoNLL-2002. In Sect. 7.6, we detail the application of ETL for the DUT CoNLL-2002. Finally, Sect. 7.7 presents some concluding remarks.

Keywords Machine learning · Natural language processing · Named entity recognition · Entropy guided transformation learning · ETL committee · Transformation based learning · Adaboost

7.1 Task and Corpora

Named entity recognition is the problem of finding all proper nouns in a text and to classify them among several given categories of interest. Usually, there are three given categories: Person, Organization and Location. In the example that follows, we use brackets to indicate the four named entities in the sentence.

```
[PER Wolff ], currently a journalist in [LOC Argentina
], played with [PER Del Bosque ] in the final years of
             the seventies in [ORG Real Madrid ]
```

C. N. dos Santos and R. L. Milidiú, *Entropy Guided Transformation Learning:*
Algorithms and Applications, SpringerBriefs in Computer Science,
DOI: 10.1007/978-1-4471-2978-3_7, © The Author(s) 2012

Table 7.1 Named entity recognition corpora

Corpus	Language	Training data		Test data	
		Sentenc.	Tokens	Sentenc.	Tokens
HAREM	Portuguese	4,749	98,475	3,393	66,627
SPA CoNLL-2002	Spanish	8,323	264,715	1,517	51,533
DUT CoNLL-2002	Dutch	15,806	202,931	5,195	68,994

We apply ETL to three different NER corpora in three different languages. The selected corpora are: HAREM [5], a Portuguese NER corpus; SPA CoNLL-2002 [7], a Spanish NER corpus; and DUT CoNLL-2002 [7], a Dutch NER corpus. Table 7.1 shows some characteristics of the three selected corpora.

The HAREM Corpus is a golden set for NER in Portuguese [5]. This corpus is annotated with ten named entity categories: Person (PESSOA), Organization (ORGANIZACAO), Location (LOCAL), Value (VALOR), Date (TEMPO), Abstraction (ABSTRACCAO), Title (OBRA), Event (ACONTECIMENTO), Thing (COISA) and Other (VARIADO). Additionally, we automatically generate the *POS* feature. We use the ETL POS tagger trained with the Mac-Morpho Corpus to create the *POS* feature. The HAREM corpus is already divided into two sets. Each set corresponds to a different Portuguese NER contest [5]. Here, we use the data from the first contest as the training set. The data from the second contest, which is called MiniHAREM, is our test set.

Both SPA CoNLL-2002 Corpus and DUT CoNLL-2002 Corpus were used in the CoNLL-2002 shared task [7]. They are annotated with four named entity categories: Person, Organization, Location and Miscellaneous. These corpora are also annotated with *POS* tags. The CONLL-2002 corpora are already divided into training and test sets. They also include development corpora which have characteristics similar to the test corpora. The development set is used to tune parameters of the learning systems.

In the three corpora, the *NE tags* feature provides the named entity annotation. The *NE tags* feature uses the IOB1 tagging style, where: O, means that the word is not a NE; I-X, means that the word is part of a NE type X and B-X is used for the leftmost word of a NE beginning immediately after another NE of the same type. The IOB1 tagging style is illustrated in the following example.

```
Wolff/I-PER  ,/O  currently/O  a/O  journalist/O  in/O
Argentina/I-PLA  ,/O  played/O  with/O  Del/I-PER
   Bosque/I-PER  in/O  the/O  final/O  years/O  of/O
   the/O  seventies/O  in/O  Real/I-ORG  Madrid/I-ORG
```

7.2 Named Entity Recognition Modeling

Our named entity recognition approach for the two CoNLL-2002 corpora follows the two stages strategy used in the training of ETL POS taggers (see Chap. 5). As in the POS tagging experiments, we use ETL for the learning of contextual rules only.

For the HAREM Corpus, we use ETL to classify only the five most frequent categories: Person, Organization, Location, Date and Value.

When performing NER, at both training and test time, we generate some *derived features*. This step is performed before the training and test time. It is described in the following subsection.

7.2.1 Derived Features

The training and test corpora provide three input features: *word*, *POS* and *NE tags*. Using the input features, we produce the following four derived features:

- **Capitalization**: this feature classify the words according to their capitalization. It assumes one the following categorical values: First Letter is Uppercase, All Letters are Uppercase, All Letters are Lowercase, Number, Punctuation, Number with "/" or "-" inside or Other.
- **Dictionary membership**: this feature classify the words according to their presence in a dictionary. It assumes one the following categorical values: Upper, Lower, Both or None. For the corpora DUT CoNLL-2002 and SPA CoNLL-2002, the dictionary consists of the words appearing in their respective training sets. For the HAREM Corpus, the dictionary consists of the words appearing in the MAC-Morpho Corpus. We use the MAC-Morpho Corpus because its vocabulary is larger than the one of the HAREM Corpus.
- **Word length**: this feature classify the words according to their lengths. It assumes one the following categorical values: 1, 2, 3, 4, 5, 6–8 or >8.
- **Noun phrases**: this feature is generated using the ETL NP Chunker trained with the SNR-CLIC Corpus. We generate this feature only for the HAREM Corpus.

7.3 Machine Learning Modeling

The following ML model configurations provide our best results.

BLS: for the HAREM Corpus, we apply a BLS that makes use of gazetteers only. We use the gazetteers presented in [4], as well as some sections of the REPENTINO gazetteer [6]. From the REPENTINO gazetteer we use only the categories Beings, Location and Organization. We use only some subcategories of the REPENTINO gazetteer. From category Beings we use subcategory Human. From Location we use Terrestrial, Town, Region and Adm. Division. From Organization we use all subcategories. For some subcategories an extra processing is also required. From Human, we extract only first names. From the Organization category, we use full company names and extract the top 100 most frequent words. We also use a month name gazetteer and a list of lower case words that can start a NE.

For both SPA and DUT CoNLL 2002 corpora, the baseline system assigns to each word the *NE tag* that was most frequently associated with that word in the training set. If capitalized, an unknown word is tagged as a person, otherwise it is tagged as non entity.

TBL: for the HAREM Corpus, the reported results for the TBL approach refer to TBL trained with the 32 handcrafted template set proposed by Milidiú et al. [4]. For the two CoNLL 2002 corpora, we use the Brill's template set [2].

ETL: in the ETL learning, for the three corpora, we use the features *word*, *POS*, *NE tags*, *capitalization information*, *dictionary membership* and *word length*. For the HAREM Corpus, we additionally use the *noun phrase* feature. The default ETL parameter setting shown in Sect. 4.2 is used.

ETL$_{TE}$: we use the same ETL configuration, but here we perform template evolution.

ETL$_{CMT}$: we use the default ETL committee parametrization shown in Sect. 4.3.

We also report the state-of-the-art system performance for each corpus.

In order to assess the system performances over the two CoNLL-2002 corpora, we use the evaluation tool provided in the CoNLL-2002 website [7]. For the HAREM Corpus, we use the evaluation tools described in [5].

7.4 HAREM Corpus

As Santos and Cardoso [5], we report the category classification results in two scenarios: total and selective. In the *total scenario*, all the categories are taken into account when scoring the systems. In the *selective scenario*, only the five chosen categories (Person, Organization, Location, Date and Value) are taken into account.

Here, our test corpus corresponds to the data used in the second Portuguese NER contest, the MiniHAREM [5]. For this test corpus, the CORTEX system [1] shows the best result reported so far. According to Aranha [1], the CORTEX system relies in the use of handcrafted rules that jointly work with a rich knowledge base for the NER task. Here, we also list the CORTEX system performance reported by Aranha.

In Tables 7.2 and 7.3, we summarize the system performance results for the total and selective scenarios, respectively. For the total scenario, the ETL system reduces the BLS $F_{\beta=1}$ error by 39%, from 64.26 to 39.18. In both scenarios, ETL and CORTEX have similar results. In both tables, we can see that ETL significantly outperforms the TBL system. Using template evolution, the training time is reduced by nearly 35% and there is no performance loss. Actually, the ETL$_{TE}$ system has a $F_{\beta=1}$ slightly better than the one of ETL. In both scenarios, ETL$_{CMT}$ achieves the best $F_{\beta=1}$. In the total scenario, the ETL$_{CMT}$ system reduces the $F_{\beta=1}$ error by 7% when compared to the single ETL system. As far as we know, ETL$_{CMT}$ results are the best reported so far for named entity classification of the HAREM Corpus.

The TBL results for the HAREM Corpus are very poor due to its template set, which is the same used with the LearnNEC06 Corpus proposed in [4]. This is the only

Table 7.2 System performances in the total scenario for the HAREM corpus

System	Precision (%)	Recall (%)	$F_{\beta=1}$	# Templates
ETL$_{CMT}$	77.52	**53.86**	**63.56**	50
CORTEX	**77.85**	50.92	61.57	–
ETL$_{TE}$	74.92	51.90	61.32	87
ETL	71.08	53.15	60.82	87
TBL	57.78	45.20	50.72	32
BLS	47.87	28.52	35.74	–

Table 7.3 System performances in the selective scenario for the HAREM corpus

System	Precision (%)	Recall (%)	$F_{\beta=1}$	# Templates
ETL$_{CMT}$	77.27	**65.20**	**70.72**	50
CORTEX	**77.86**	60.97	68.39	–
ETL$_{TE}$	74.75	62.82	68.27	87
ETL	70.90	64.34	67.46	87
TBL	57.76	54.69	56.19	32
BLS	47.85	34.52	40.11	–

Table 7.4 ETL$_{CMT}$ results by entity type for the HAREM corpus

Entity	Precision (%)	Recall (%)	$F_{\beta=1}$
Date	88.29	82.21	85.14
Location	76.18	68.16	71.95
Organization	65.34	50.29	56.84
Person	81.49	61.14	69.87
Vale	77.72	70.13	73.73
Overall	77.27	65.20	70.72

TBL template set that we have found for the Portuguese NER task. This template set contains some pre-instantiated tests, therefore it seems to be very restricted to the kind of named entity structures that appear in the LearnNEC06 Corpus.

In Table 7.4, we show the ETL$_{CMT}$ system results, broken down by named entity type, for the HAREM Corpus. The best result is obtained for the *Date* category, where a precision of 88.29% is achieved. This is mainly because most of the NEs in this category follow very simple and fixed patterns such as "the [*a day*] of [*a month*]". The NE *Organization* is the most difficult one to extract. We believe that this difficulty comes mainly from two facts: (1) the length of organization names is more dynamic. For instance, in the HAREM Corpus some organization names are composed by more than seven words; and (2) the recognition of organization name abbreviations is a hard task.

Like any other ML based strategy, the versatility of ETL based systems is one advantage over other non-ML based systems, such as CORTEX. All the used resources, but the training set and gazetteers, are language independent. As we show in the next two sections, we can quickly create an ETL based NER system for any language that has an available training set.

7.5 SPA CoNLL-2002 Corpus

Carreras et al. [3] present an AdaBoost system with state-of-the-art performance for the SPA CoNLL-2002 Corpus. Their AdaBoost system uses decision trees as a base learner. Therefore, for the SPA CoNLL-2002 Corpus, we also list the AdaBoost system performance reported by Carreras et al.

In Table 7.5, we summarize the system performance results. The ETL system reduces the BLS $F_{\beta=1}$ error by 47%, from 44.49 to 23.72. For the SPA CoNLL-2002 Corpus, ETL significantly outperforms TBL. The ETL_{TE} system reduces the ETL training time by 57%, from 26.3 to 11.3 min. However, there is a performance loss in terms of $F_{\beta=1}$. The ETL_{CMT} system reduces the $F_{\beta=1}$ error by 5% when compared to the single ETL system.

Through a quick analysis of the results, we found out that the majority of errors are related to *names* that do not occur in the training corpus. This result suggests that the use of gazetteers has the potential to improve the ETL results.

Although the ETL system has a $F_{\beta=1}$ smaller than the one of the AdaBoost system, the ETL modeling phase seems to be simpler than the one of the Carreras et al.'s system. They divide the NER task into two intermediate tasks: NE identification and NE classification. In the first stage, the AdaBoost system identifies NE candidates. In the second stage, the AdaBoost system classify the identified candidates. Our ETL approach for NER is more straightforward, since we do not divide the task. Nevertheless, for the SPA CoNLL-2002, the ETL committee system is in top three when compared with the 12 CoNLL-2002 contestant systems.

In Table 7.6, we show the ETL_{CMT} system results, broken down by named entity type, for the SPA CoNLL-2002 Corpus.

7.6 DUT CoNLL-2002 Corpus

The Carreras et al. [3] AdaBoost based system is also a state-of-the-art system for the DUT CoNLL-2002 Corpus. Therefore, for the DUT CoNLL-2002 Corpus, we also list the AdaBoost system performance reported by Carreras et al.

In Table 7.7, we summarize the system performance results. The ETL system reduces the BLS $F_{\beta=1}$ error by 47%, from 48.58 to 25.82. For the DUT CoNLL-2002 Corpus, ETL significantly outperforms TBL. The ETL_{TE} system reduces the ETL training time by 55%, from 15.5 to 7 min. However, there is a performance loss in terms of $F_{\beta=1}$. The ETL_{CMT} system reduces the $F_{\beta=1}$ error by 5% when compared to the single ETL system.

As in the SPA CoNLL-2002 Corpus, the majority of errors are related to *names* that do not occur in the training corpus. Therefore, we believe that the use of gazetteers has also the potential to improve the ETL results for the DUT CoNLL-2002 Corpus.

Table 7.5 System performances for the SPA CoNLL-2002 corpus

System	Precision (%)	Recall (%)	$F_{\beta=1}$	# Templates
AdaBoost	**79.27**	**79.29**	**79.28**	–
ETL$_{CMT}$	76.99	77.94	77.46	50
ETL	75.50	77.07	76.28	98
ETL$_{TE}$	74.28	75.64	74.95	98
TBL	72.27	74.99	73.61	26
BLS	49.59	63.02	55.51	–

Table 7.6 ETL$_{CMT}$ results by entity type for the SPA CoNLL-2002 corpus

Entity	Precision (%)	Recall (%)	$F_{\beta=1}$
Location	80.75	75.83	78.21
Miscellaneous	54.06	50.88	52.42
Organization	76.01	80.57	78.22
Person	83.35	88.57	85.88
Overall	76.99	77.94	77.46

Table 7.7 System performances for the DUT CoNLL-2002 corpus

System	Precision (%)	Recall (%)	$F_{\beta=1}$	# Templates
AdaBoost	**77.83**	**76.29**	**77.05**	–
ETL$_{CMT}$	76.52	74.38	75.44	50
ETL	74.97	73.39	74.18	79
ETL$_{TE}$	73.96	72.33	73.14	79
TBL	69.42	72.05	70.71	26
BLS	47.68	55.80	51.42	–

Table 7.8 ETL$_{CMT}$ results by entity type for the DUT CoNLL-2002 corpus

Entity	Precision (%)	Recall (%)	$F_{\beta=1}$
Location	79.77	80.80	80.28
Miscellaneous	72.51	69.33	70.89
Organization	78.80	62.71	69.84
Person	76.87	84.60	80.55
Overall	76.52	74.38	75.44

Similarly to the SPA CoNLL-2002 Corpus, the Carreras et al.'s system divide the NER task into two intermediate tasks: NE identification and NE classification. In the first stage, the AdaBoost system identifies NE candidates. In the second stage, the AdaBoost system classify the identified candidates. Our ETL approach for NER is more straightforward, since we do not divide the task. Nevertheless, for the DUT CoNLL-2002, the ETL committee system is in top two when compared with the 12 CoNLL-2002 contestant systems.

In Table 7.8, we show the ETL$_{CMT}$ system results, broken down by named entity type, for the DUT CoNLL-2002 Corpus.

7.7 Summary

This chapter presents the application of ETL to language independent named entity recognition. We apply ETL to three different corpora in three different languages. The selected corpora are: HAREM, a Portuguese NER corpus; SPA CoNLL-2002, a Spanish NER corpus; and DUT CoNLL-2002, a Dutch NER corpus.

Using the default parameter setting and a common set of features, the ETL system achieves state-of-the-art competitive results for the three corpora. ETL outperforms TBL with handcrafted templates in all the experiments. This finding indicates that the entropy guided template generation employed by ETL is very effective for the NER task.

The rule application phase of ETL NER systems is fast. For instance, our Python implementation of the ETL NER created with the HAREM Corpus processes about 9,500 tokens per second. The template evolution strategy provides a reasonable reduction of training time in the three corpora. However, for both SPA CONLL-2002 Corpus and DUT CONLL-2002 Corpus the template evolution reduces the ETL $F_{\beta=1}$.

ETL committee significantly improves the ETL results for the three corpora. For the HAREM Corpus, ETL committee achieves the best result reported so far. Training a committee of 100 classifiers using the SPA CONLL-2002 Corpus takes about two hours on our 30 CPU-core cluster.

These chapter results indicate that ETL and ETL committee are effective methods to produce competitive language independent NER systems with little modeling effort.

References

1. Aranha, C.N.: Reconhecimento de entidades mencionadas em português, chap. O Cortex e a sua participação no HAREM. Linguateca, Portugal (2007)
2. Brill, E.: Transformation-based error-driven learning and natural language processing: a case study in part-of-speech tagging. Comput. Linguist. **21**(4), 543–565 (1995)
3. Carreras, X., Màrques, L., Padró, L.: Named entity extraction using adaboost. In: Proceedings of the Conference on Computational Natural Language Learning, pp. 167–170. Taipei, Taiwan (2002)
4. Milidiú, R.L., Duarte, J.C., Cavalcante, R.: Machine learning algorithms for portuguese named entity recognition. In: Proceedings of Fourth Workshop in Information and Human Language Technology. Ribeirão Preto, Brazil (2006)
5. Santos, D., Cardoso, N.: Reconhecimento de entidades mencionadas em português. Linguateca, Portugal (2007)
6. Sarmento, L., Sofia, A., Cabral, L.: Repentino—a wide-scope gazetteer for entity recognition in portuguese. In: Proceedings of 7th Workshop on Computational Processing of Written and Spoken Portuguese, pp. 31–40. Itatiaia, Brazil (2006)
7. Tjong Kim Sang, E.F.: Introduction to the conll-2002 shared task: language-independent named entity recognition. In: Proceedings of CoNLL-2002, pp. 155–158. Taipei, Taiwan (2002)

Chapter 8
Semantic Role Labeling

Abstract This chapter presents the application of the ETL approach to semantic role labeling (SRL). The SRL task consists in detecting basic event structures in a given text. Some of these event structures include *who* did *what* to *whom*, *when* and *where*. We evaluate the performance of ETL over two English language corpora: CoNLL-2004 and CoNLL-2005. ETL system achieves regular results for the two corpora. However, for the CoNLL-2004 Corpus, our ETL system outperforms the TBL system proposed by Higgins [4]. ETL committee significantly improves the ETL results for the two corpora. This chapter is organized as follows. In Sect. 8.1, we describe the selected corpora. In Sect. 8.2, we detail some modeling configurations used in our SRL system. In Sect. 8.3, we show some configurations used in the machine learning algorithms. Section 8.4 presents the application of ETL for the CoNLL-2004 Corpus. Section 8.5 presents the application of ETL for the CoNLL-2005 Corpus. Finally, Sect. 8.6 presents some concluding remarks.

Keywords Machine learning · Natural language processing · Semantic role labeling · Entropy guided transformation learning · ETL committee · Transformation based learning · Support vector machines · Adaboost

8.1 Task and Corpora

Semantic role labeling is the process of detecting basic event structures such as *who* did *what* to *whom*, *when* and *where* [9]. The SRL task is performed at the sentence-level. More specifically, for each predicate of a clause, whose head is typically a verb, all the constituents in the sentence which fill a semantic role of the verb have to be recognized. Typical semantic roles, also called arguments, include Agent, Patient, Instrument, and also adjuncts such as Locative, Temporal, Manner, and Cause [1]. A verb and its set of arguments form a *proposition* in the sentence. SRL provides a key knowledge that helps to build more elaborated document management and

C. N. dos Santos and R. L. Milidiú, *Entropy Guided Transformation Learning:*
Algorithms and Applications, SpringerBriefs in Computer Science,
DOI: 10.1007/978-1-4471-2978-3_8, © The Author(s) 2012

Table 8.1 Semantic role labeling corpora

Corpus	Language	Training data		Test data	
		Sentenc.	Tokens	Sentenc.	Tokens
CoNLL-2004	English	8,936	211,727	1,671	40,039
CoNLL-2005	English	39,832	950,028	2,416	56,684

information extraction applications. The following sentence illustrates this labeling task.

> [*A0* He] [*AM-MOD* would] [*AM-NEG* n't] [*V* accept]
> [*A1* anything of value] from [*A2* those he was
>   writing about] .

Here, the semantic roles of the predicate *accept* are marked with the labels: V=*verb*; A0=*acceptor*; A1=*thing accepted*; A2=*accepted-from*; AM-MOD=*modal*; AM-NEG=*negation*.

We evaluate the performance of ETL over two English language corpora: CoNLL-2004 [1] and CoNLL-2005 [2]. These two corpora were used in the CoNLL shared task of the years 2004 and 2005, respectively. Table 8.1 shows some characteristics of these corpora.

The CoNLL-2005 Corpus consists of the Proposition Bank (PropBank) [7], an approximately one-million-word corpus annotated with predicate-argument structures. The PropBank annotates the Wall Street Journal part of the Penn TreeBank [5] with verb argument structure. The CoNLL-2005 Corpus is already divided into training and test sets. The Penn TreeBank sections 02–21 are used for training. Additionally, section 23 is used for test. Section 24 is used as a development set, to tune parameters of the learning systems. The CoNLL-2004 Corpus is a subset of the CoNLL-2005 Corpus. It uses Penn TreeBank sections 15–18 for training and section 21 for test. In the CoNLL-2004 Corpus, section 20 is used as a development set.

The SRL corpora are annotated with four basic input features: *POS tags*, *phrase chunks*, *clauses* and *named entities*. *Clauses* are word sequences which contain a subject and a predicate. The *clause* feature indicates when a token begins or ends a clause. These four input features were automatically generated using state-of-the-art systems [2]. The SRL corpora also include two other features: the *target verbs* feature, which indicates the verbs whose arguments must be labeled; and the *srl tags* feature, which provides the semantic labeling.

The *srl tags* used in the PropBank annotation numbers the arguments of each predicate from A0 to A5. Usually, A0 stands for agent, A1 for theme or direct object, and A2 for indirect object, benefactive or instrument, but semantics tend to be verb specific [9]. Adjunctive arguments are referred to as AM-T, where T is the type of the adjunct. For instance, AM-MNR indicates manner, AM-TMP indicates a temporal, and AM-LOC indicates a locative. Arguments can be discontinuous, in which case the continuation fragments are prefixed by C-, for instance, "*[A1 The economy], [A0 he] [V noted], [C-A1 moves the market], not vice versa*". In the PropBank annotation,

Bob	NNP	B-NP	(S*	B-PER	–	(A0*	*
Stone	NNP	I-NP	*	I-PER	–	*A0)	*
stewed	VBD	B-VP	*	O	stew	(V*V)	*
over	IN	B-PP	*	O	–	*	*
a	DT	B-NP	*	O	–	(A1*	(A0*
letter	NN	I-NP	*	O	–	*	*
from	IN	B-PP	*	O	–	*	*
his	PRP$	B-NP	*	O	–	*	*
manager	NN	I-NP	*	O	–	*	*A0)
putting	VBG	B-VP	*	O	put	*	(V*V)
him	PRP	B-NP	*	O	–	*	(A1*A1)
on	IN	B-PP	*	O	–	*	*
probation	NN	B-NP	*	O	–	*	(A2*A2)
for	IN	B-PP	*	O	–	*	(AM-CAU*
insubordination	NN	B-NP	*	O	–	*A1)	*AM-CAU)
.	.	O	*S)	O	–	*	*

Fig. 8.1 Example of an annotated sentence from the CoNLL 2004 corpus

argument references share the same label with the actual argument prefixed with R-. References are typically pronominal.

In Fig. 8.1, we show an annotated sentence from the CoNLL 2004 Corpus. The input columns consists of words (1st), POS tags (2nd), base chunks (3rd), clauses (4th) and named entities (5th). The 6th column marks target verbs, and their propositions are found in 7th and 8th columns. According to the PropBank annotation, for *stew* (7th), the A0 annotates the *worrier*, and the A1 the *cause*. For *put* (8th), the A0 annotates the *putter*, A1 is the *thing put*, and A2 the *where put*.

The CoNLL-2005 Corpus also includes *full parsing* features, the complete syntactic trees given by two alternative parsers. This kind of feature eases the semantic role labeling task [8]. However, since our purpose is to examine the ETL performance for a complex task, we do not use the full parsing features in our SRL experiments. Therefore, the same system configuration is used for both corpora.

8.2 Semantic Role Labeling Modeling

We approach the SRL task as a token classification problem. Which means that, for each token, the system must decide when the token starts or ends a specific kind of argument.

When performing SRL, at both training and test time, we have three additional steps: generation of derived features, preprocessing and postprocessing. The preprocessing and generation of derived features are performed before the training and test time. The postprocessing is executed after the training and test time. These three steps are described in the following subsections.

8.2.1 Derived Features

The training and test corpora provide six input features: *word*, *POS*, *named entities*, *phrase chunks*, *clauses*, *target verbs* and *SRL tags*. Using the input features, we produce the following thirteen derived features:

- **Token Position**: indicates if the token comes before or after the target verb.
- **Temporal**: indicates if the word is or not a temporal keyword. The temporal keywords list contains the words that frequently appear as temporal adjuncts in the training set, such as the words *December*, *Monday* and *since*.
- **Path**: the sequence of chunk tags between the chunk and the target verb. Consecutive NP chunks are treated as one.
- **Pathlex**: the same as the *path* feature with the exception that here we use the preposition itself instead of the PP chunk tag.
- **Distance**: the number of chunks between the chunk and the target verb. Consecutive NP chunks are also treated as one.
- **VP Distance**: distance, in number of VP chunks, between the token and the target verb.
- **Clause Path**: the clause bracket chain between the token and the target verb.
- **Clause Position**: indicates if the token is inside or outside of the clause which contains the target verb.
- **Number of Predicates**: number of target verbs in the sentence.
- **Voice**: indicates the target verb voice: active or passive.
- **Target Verb POS**: POS tag of the target verb.
- **Predicate POS Context**: the POS tags of the words that immediately precede and follow the predicate. The POS tag of a preposition is replaced with the preposition itself.
- **Predicate Argument Patterns**: for each predicate, we identify the most frequent left and right patterns of the core arguments (A0 through A5) in the training set. For instance, *separate* has A0 and A1_A2 as its most frequent left and right argument patterns, respectively. For the *separate* verb, this feature assumes the value A0 for the tokens on the left side of the verb, and the value A1_A2 for the tokens on the right side.

All these features were previously used in other SRL systems [3, 6]. For those systems, these features prove to be very important for performance improvement.

8.2.2 Preprocessing

We use a different token representation for the SRL task. Here, our system classifies phrase chunks instead of words. Which means that here a token represents a complete phrase chunk. In the preprocessing step, the original word-based tokens are collapsed in order to generate the new representation. In the collapsing process, only the feature

Stone	NNP	I-NP	(S*	I-PER	–	(A0*A0)	*
stewed	VBD	B-VP	*	O	stew	(V*V)	*
over	IN	B-PP	*	O	–	*	*
letter	NN	I-NP	*	O	–	(A1*	(A0*
from	IN	B-PP	*	O	–	*	*
manager	NN	I-NP	*	O	–	*	*A0)
putting	VBG	B-VP	*	O	put	*	(V*V)
him	PRP	B-NP	*	O	–	*	(A1*A1)
on	IN	B-PP	*	O	–	*	*
probation	NN	B-NP	*	O	–	*	(A2*A2)
for	IN	B-PP	*	O	–	*	(AM-CAU*
insubordination	NN	B-NP	*	O	–	*A1)	*AM-CAU)
.	.	O	*S)	O	–	*	*

Fig. 8.2 Example of a sentence in the collapsed tokens version

values of the phrase chunk headwords are retained. The chunk headword is defined as its rightmost word. This preprocessing speeds up the training step, since the number of tokens to be annotated are reduced. As a consequence, larger sentence segments are covered with smaller context window sizes. In Fig. 8.2 we show the collapsed version of the sentence shown in Fig. 8.1. In this example, the chunks "*Bob Stone*", "*a letter*" and "*his manager*" are collapsed.

We treat propositions independently. Therefore, for each target verb we generate a separate sequence of tokens to be annotated. In general, all the arguments of a proposition are inside the target verb clause. Hence, we do not include tokens that are outside of the target verb clause. The only exception is when we have a nested clause that begins with a target verb. Here, we must also include the external clause.

In Fig. 8.3, we show the token sequences for the two target verbs shown in Fig. 8.2. Note that, for this particular case, the token sequences for each verb are the same. Only the two last columns, which defines the target verb and the proposition annotation, are verb specific.

8.2.3 Postprocessing

During the postprocess step, some constraints are added to the extracted arguments. These constraints remove simple mistakes by removing or editing identified arguments. The following constraints and corresponding editions are implemented.

- There can be only one argument A[0–5] per sentence. If more than one is found, we keep only the target verb closest argument, all the others being removed.
- An argument can not have its boundaries outside the clause it starts. Otherwise, the argument would have its boundaries cropped to fit the clause boundaries.

```
Stone              NNP  I-NP   (S*    I-PER   -      (A0*A0)
stewed             VBD  B-VP    *     O      stew    (V*V)
over               IN   B-PP    *     O       -       *
letter             NN   I-NP    *     O       -      (A1*
from               IN   B-PP    *     O       -       *
manager            NN   I-NP    *     O       -       *
putting            VBG  B-VP    *     O       -       *
him                PRP  B-NP    *     O       -       *
on                 IN   B-PP    *     O       -       *
probation          NN   B-NP    *     O       -       *
for                IN   B-PP    *     O       -       *
insubordination    NN   B-NP    *     O       -      *A1)
.                  .    O      *S)    O       -       *

Stone              NNP  I-NP   (S*    I-PER   -              *
stewed             VBD  B-VP    *     O       -              *
over               IN   B-PP    *     O       -              *
letter             NN   I-NP    *     O       -          (A0*
from               IN   B-PP    *     O       -             *
manager            NN   I-NP    *     O       -          *A0)
putting            VBG  B-VP    *     O      put       (V*V)
him                PRP  B-NP    *     O       -       (A1*A1)
on                 IN   B-PP    *     O       -             *
probation          NN   B-NP    *     O       -       (A2*A2)
for                IN   B-PP    *     O       -      (AM-CAU*
insubordination    NN   B-NP    *     O       -       *AM-CAU)
.                  .    O      *S)    O       -             *
```

Fig. 8.3 Token sequences for the target verbs *stew* and *put*

8.3 Machine Learning Modeling

We use the following task specific configurations.

BLS: we use the same baseline system proposed for the CoNLL-2004 Shared Task [1]. It is based on six heuristic rules that make use of POS and phrase chunks:

1. Tag *not* and *n't* in target verb chunk as AM-NEG.
2. Tag *modal verbs* in target verb chunk as AM-MOD.
3. Tag first NP before target verb as A0.
4. Tag first NP after target verb as A1.
5. Tag *that*, *which* and *who* before target verb as R-A0.
6. Switch A0 and A1, and R-A0 and R-A1 if the target verb is part of a passive VP chunk.

TBL: we do not use handcrafted TBL templates for the SRL task. Therefore, we only present the TBL results for the CoNLL-2004 corpora reported by Higgins [4]. Higgins used a set of 133 templates which reference basic and derived features.

ETL: in the ETL learning, we use all the input and derived features. The default ETL parameter setting shown in Sect. 4.2 is used.

ETL$_{TE}$: we use the same ETL configuration, but here we perform template evolution.

Table 8.2 System performances for the CoNLL-2004 corpus

System	Precision (%)	Recall (%)	$F_{\beta=1}$	# Templates
SVM	72.43	**66.77**	**69.49**	–
ETL$_{CMT}$	**76.44**	60.25	67.39	50
ETL	70.60	57.48	63.37	632
ETL$_{TE}$	69.41	56.85	62.50	632
TBL	64.17	57.52	60.66	130
BLS	55.57	30.58	39.45	–

ETL$_{CMT}$: we use the default ETL committee parametrization shown in Sect. 4.3.

We also report the state-of-the-art system performance for each corpus.

In order to assess the system performances on the CoNLL-2004 Corpus, we use the evaluation tool provided in the CoNLL-2004 website [1]. For the CoNLL-2005 Corpus, we use the evaluation tool provided in the CoNLL-2005 website [2].

8.4 CoNLL-2004 Corpus

Hacioglu et al. [3] present a SVM-based system that does not use full parsing. This system achieves state-of-the-art performance for the CoNLL-2004 Corpus. Therefore, for this Corpus, we also list the SVM system performance reported by Hacioglu et al.

In Table 8.2, we summarize the system performance results. The ETL system reduces the BLS $F_{\beta=1}$ error by 40%, from 60.55 to 36.63. Our ETL system reduces the $F_{\beta=1}$ error by 7% when compared to the Higgins's TBL system. The ETL$_{TE}$ system reduces the ETL training time by 78%, from 10 to 2.2 h. However, there is a performance loss in terms of $F_{\beta=1}$. The lengthy training time is due to the large number of generated templates. For this corpus, ETL generates 632 templates.

The postprocessing step has very little impact in the final performance. For the ETL system, the postprocessing improves the $F_{\beta=1}$ by only 0.3.

The ETL$_{CMT}$ system reduces the $F_{\beta=1}$ error by 11% when compared to the single ETL system. ETL$_{CMT}$ performance is very competitive with the one of the SVM system. Moreover, the precision error of the ETL$_{CMT}$ system is 15% smaller than the one of the SVM system. As far as we know, the precision of the ETL$_{CMT}$, 76.44, is the best one reported so far for a system that does not use full or joint parsing. In most situations, precision is more important than recall. Nevertheless, for the CoNLL-2004, the ETL committee system is in top two when compared with the 10 CoNLL-2004 contestant systems.

In Table 8.3 we show the ETL$_{CMT}$ system results, broken down by argument type, for the CoNLL-2004 Corpus. Among the core arguments, A1-A5, the best results are for A0 and A1, which are the most frequent ones. Among the adjuncts, the best results are for AM-MOD, modal, and AM-NEG, negation, which follow very simple fixed patterns.

Table 8.3 ETL$_{CMT}$ results by argument type for the CoNLL-2004 corpus

	Precision (%)	Recall (%)	F$_{\beta=1}$
Overall	76.44	60.25	67.39
A0	86.19	68.98	76.63
A1	75.69	66.84	70.99
A2	59.92	43.98	50.73
A3	52.63	33.33	40.82
A4	70.73	58.00	63.74
A5	0.00	0.00	0.00
AA	0.00	0.00	0.00
AM-ADV	53.09	28.01	36.67
AM-CAU	40.00	16.33	23.19
AM-DIR	32.00	16.00	21.33
AM-DIS	71.35	57.28	63.54
AM-EXT	57.14	57.14	57.14
AM-LOC	46.49	23.25	30.99
AM-MNR	56.36	24.31	33.97
AM-MOD	99.68	92.58	96.00
AM-NEG	94.57	96.06	95.31
AM-PNC	44.44	9.41	15.53
AM-PRD	0.00	0.00	0.00
AM-TMP	73.08	48.33	58.18
R-A0	85.62	78.62	81.97
R-A1	78.72	52.86	63.25
R-A2	44.44	44.44	44.44
R-A3	0.00	0.00	0.00
R-AA	0.00	0.00	0.00
R-AM-LOC	100.00	25.00	40.00
R-AM-MNR	0.00	0.00	0.00
R-AM-PNC	0.00	0.00	0.00
R-AM-TMP	66.67	14.29	23.53
V	98.07	98.07	98.07

Table 8.4 System performances for the CoNLL-2005 corpus

System	Precision (%)	Recall (%)	F$_{\beta=1}$	# Templates
AdaBoost	78.76	**72.44**	**75.47**	–
ETL$_{CMT}$	**80.54**	65.47	72.23	50
ETL	76.79	64.45	70.08	434
ETL$_{TE}$	74.75	63.27	68.53	632
BLS	51.33	27.88	36.14	–

8.5 CoNLL-2005 Corpus

Surdeanu et al. [9] present an AdaBoost-based system that does not use full parsing. This system, as far as we know, achieves the best reported performance for the CoNLL-2005 Corpus when full parsing is not considered. Therefore, for this Corpus, we also list the AdaBoost system performance reported by Surdeanu et al.

Table 8.5 ETL$_{CMT}$ results by argument type for the CoNLL-2005 corpus

Datalabel	Precision(%)	Recall(%)	$F_{\beta=1}$
Overall	80.54	65.47	72.23
A0	88.47	70.84	78.68
A1	78.43	69.88	73.91
A2	67.12	57.57	61.98
A3	69.23	41.62	51.99
A4	70.83	66.67	68.69
A5	50.00	100.00	66.67
AA	0.00	0.00	0.00
AM-ADV	71.90	34.39	46.52
AM-CAU	70.97	30.14	42.31
AM-DIR	53.97	40.00	45.95
AM-DIS	82.04	62.81	71.15
AM-EXT	72.73	50.00	59.26
AM-LOC	63.93	38.57	48.11
AM-MNR	64.47	42.73	51.40
AM-MOD	98.86	94.19	96.47
AM-NEG	99.10	96.09	97.57
AM-PNC	60.53	20.00	30.07
AM-PRD	0.00	0.00	0.00
AM-REC	0.00	0.00	0.00
AM-TMP	80.10	58.51	67.62
R-A0	90.26	78.57	84.01
R-A1	78.99	69.87	74.15
R-A2	58.33	43.75	50.00
R-A3	0.00	0.00	0.00
R-A4	0.00	0.00	0.00
R-AM-ADV	0.00	0.00	0.00
R-AM-CAU	100.00	25.00	40.00
R-AM-EXT	0.00	0.00	0.00
R-AM-LOC	85.71	28.57	42.86
R-AM-MNR	50.00	33.33	40.00
R-AM-TMP	79.49	59.62	68.13
V	98.90	98.90	98.90

Due to memory restrictions, we train the ETL system using templates that combine at most five features. However, for the ETL$_{TE}$ system we can use all the templates, since this training strategy uses less memory. In Table 8.4, we summarize the system performance results. The ETL system reduces the BLS $F_{\beta=1}$ error by 53%, from 63.86 to 29.92. Even using a larger template set, the ETL$_{TE}$ system reduces the ETL training time by 63%. Nevertheless, there is a performance loss in terms of $F_{\beta=1}$. This reduction in the $F_{\beta=1}$ indicates that the SRL task requires complex templates throughout the training process. The reason is that SRL is a hard task which makes use of a large number of features.

The ETL$_{CMT}$ system reduces the $F_{\beta=1}$ error by 7.2% when compared to the single ETL system. The ETL$_{CMT}$ performance is competitive with the one of the AdaBoost system. Again, the ETL$_{CMT}$ presents state-of-the-art precision performance. It is important to note that we do not use full parsing in our experiments. State-of-the-art systems using full parsing achieve $F_{\beta=1}$ of about 80% in the CoNLL-2005 test set.

In Table 8.5 we show the ETL$_{CMT}$ system results, broken down by argument type, for the CoNLL-2005 Corpus.

8.6 Summary

This chapter presents the application of the ETL approach to SRL. We evaluate the performance of ETL over two English language corpora: CoNLL-2004 and CoNLL-2005.

Using the default parameter setting and a common set of features, the ETL system achieves regular results for the two corpora. However, for the CoNLL-2004 Corpus, our ETL system outperforms the TBL system proposed by Higgins [4]. This finding indicates that, for the SRL task, the entropy guided template generation employed by ETL is more effective than the Higgins's handcrafted templates.

The classification phase of the ETL SRL systems is very fast. For instance, our Python implementation of the ETL SRL system created with the CoNLL-2005 Corpus performs the whole classification of the test set in only 30 s. The template evolution strategy provides a significant reduction of training time in the two cases. However, there is a slightly decrease in the ETL $F_{\beta=1}$.

ETL committee significantly improves the ETL results for the two corpora. When compared to the single ETL systems, ETL committee reduces the $F_{\beta=1}$ error by 11 and 7% for the CoNLL-2004 and CoNLL-2005 Corpus, respectively. We believe that the error reduction is larger for the CoNLL-2004 Corpus because this corpus is smaller. Training a committee of 100 classifiers using the CoNLL-2004 Corpus takes about ten hours on our 30 CPU-core cluster.

These chapter results indicate that ETL committee is an effective method to produce very competitive and precise SRL systems with little modeling effort. Moreover, using the ETL approach, we can produce regular SRL systems that work very fast.

References

1. Carreras, X., Màrquez, L.: Introduction to the conll-2004 shared task: semantic role labeling. In: Ng, H.T., Riloff, E. (eds.) Proceedings of the Conference on Computational Natural Language Learning, pp. 89–97. Association for Computational Linguistics, Boston, Massachusetts, USA (2004)
2. Carreras, X., Màrquez, L.: Introduction to the conll-2005 shared task: semantic role labeling. In: Proceedings of the Conference on Computational Natural Language Learning, pp. 152–164. Association for Computational Linguistics, Ann Arbor, MI, USA (2005)
3. Hacioglu, K., Pradhan, S.S., Ward, W.H., Martin, J.H., Jurafsky, D.: Semantic role labeling by tagging syntactic chunks. In: Ng, H.T., Riloff, E. (eds.) HLT-NAACL 2004 Workshop: Eighth Conference on Computational Natural Language Learning (CoNLL-2004). Association for Computational Linguistics, Boston, Massachusetts, USA (2004)

4. Higgins, D.: A transformation-based approach to argument labeling. In: Ng, H.T., Riloff, E. (eds.) HLT-NAACL 2004 Workshop: Eighth Conference on Computational Natural Language Learning (CoNLL-2004), pp. 114–117. Association for Computational Linguistics, Boston, Massachusetts, USA (2004)
5. Marcus, M.P., Marcinkiewicz, M.A., Santorini, B.: Building a large annotated corpus of english: the penn treebank. Comput. Linguist. **19**(2), 313–330 (1993)
6. Màrquez, L., Comas, P.R., Giménez, J., Català, N.: Semantic role labeling as sequential tagging. In: Proceedings of the Ninth Conference on Computational Natural, Language Learning (CONLL'05), pp. 193–196 (2005)
7. Palmer, M., Gildea, D., Kingsbury, P.: The proposition bank: an annotated corpus of semantic roles. Comput. Linguist. **31**(1), 71–106 (2005). doi:10.1162/0891201053630264
8. Punyakanok, V., Roth, D., Tau Yih, W.: The necessity of syntactic parsing for semantic role labeling. In: Proceedings of the International Joint Conference on Artificial Intelligence (IJCAI), pp. 1117–1123 (2005)
9. Surdeanu, M., Màrquez, L., Carreras, X., Comas, P.: Combination strategies for semantic role labeling. J Artif. Intell. Res. **29**, 105–151 (2007)

Chapter 9
Conclusions

Abstract Entropy guided transformation learning is a machine learning algorithm for classification tasks. In this book, we detail how ETL generalizes transformation based learning by solving the TBL bottleneck: the construction of good template sets. ETL relies on the use of the information gain measure to select feature combinations that provide effective template sets. In this work, we also present ETL committee, an ensemble method that uses ETL as the base learner. We describe the application of ETL to four language independent NLP tasks: part-of-speech tagging, phrase chunking, named entity recognition and semantic role labeling. Overall, we successfully apply it to thirteen different corpora in six different languages: Dutch, English, German, Hindi, Portuguese and Spanish. Our extensive experimental results demonstrate that ETL is an effective way to learn accurate transformation rules. In all experiments, ETL shows better results than TBL with hand-crafted templates. Our experimental results also demonstrate that ETL Committee is an effective way to improve the ETL effectiveness. We believe that by avoiding the use of hand-crafted templates, ETL enables the use of transformation rules to a greater range of classification tasks.

Keywords Machine learning · Entropy guided transformation learning · ETL committee · Transformation based learning · Natural language processing · Part-of-speech tagging · Phrase chunking · Named entity recognition · Semantic role labeling

9.1 Final Remarks on ETL

In all experimented tasks, ETL obtains results at least as good as the ones of TBL with hand-crafted templates. Based on these experimental results, we conclude that ETL effectively solves the TBL bottleneck. Moreover, for the POS tagging task, ETL obtains state-of-the-art results for the four examined corpora: Mac-Morpho, Tycho

C. N. dos Santos and R. L. Milidiú, *Entropy Guided Transformation Learning*: 71
Algorithms and Applications, SpringerBriefs in Computer Science,
DOI: 10.1007/978-1-4471-2978-3_9, © The Author(s) 2012

Brahe, TIGER and Brown. For the PCK task, ETL shows state-of-the-art results for the SNR-CLIC Corpus, and state-of-the-art competitive results for the other three examined corpora: Ramshaw and Marcus, CoNLL-2000 and SPSAL-2007. For the NER task, ETL obtains state-of-the-art competitive results for the three examined corpora: HAREM, SPA CoNLL-2002 and DUT CoNLL-2002. For the SRL task, ETL obtains regular results for the two examined corpora: CoNLL-2004 and CoNLL-2005.

We observe the following positive characteristics of the ETL approach:

1. The modeling phase is simple. It only requires a training set and a simple initial classifier. Moreover, using a common parameter setting, we achieve competitive results for language independent POS tagging, PCK, NER and SRL tasks.
2. Simplifies the use of large feature sets, since it does not require handcrafted templates. For instance, our ETL system for the SRL task uses 140 features.
3. Provides an effective way to handle high dimensional features. This property allows the use of the feature *word* in all experiments.
4. The *true class trick* allows the inclusion of the *current classification* feature in the generated templates. Hence, the TBL property of accessing intermediate results of the classification process is effectively used.
5. ETL training is reasonably fast. The observed ETL training time for the Mac-Morpho Corpus, using template evolution, is bellow one hour running on an Intel Centrino Duo 1.66 GHz notebook. The template evolution strategy also accelerates transformation learning by a factor of five for the CoNLL-2000 Corpus.
6. The classifiers produced by ETL are fast. For instance, our Python implementation of the ETL PCK created with the CoNLL-2000 Corpus processes about 12,000 tokens per second.
7. Since the ETL inputs are just the training set and the initial classifier, it is easy to use it as a base learner for an ensemble method. This is demonstrated through the ETL committee method.

9.2 Final Remarks on ETL Committee

Using the ETL committee approach, we obtain state-of-the-art competitive performance results in the thirteen corpus-driven tasks. For instance, in the PCK task, ETL committee shows state-of-the-art results for the SPSAL-2007 Corpus. For the NER task, ETL committee shows the best result reported so far for the HAREM Corpus. For the four experimented tasks, ETL committee obtains better results than the ones of single ETL models. Therefore, according to our experimental results, we conclude that ETL committee is an effective way to improve the ETL effectiveness.

We observe the following positive characteristics of the ETL committee approach:

1. Improves the ETL effectiveness without human effort.

2. Particularly useful when dealing with very complex tasks that use large sets of features. For instance, we achieve state-of-the-art competitive performance for the SRL task.
3. The training and classification processes are very easy to parallelize, since each classifier is independent from the others.

9.3 Future Work

Although ETL and ETL committee approaches present good results for the examined tasks, they can be improved by exploring the issues that we enumerate next.

1. ETL templates are restricted to the combination of *static features*. On the other hand, TBL can process templates that use *dynamic features* which are generated/updated at training time. Dynamic features are very rich and complex [2], providing a powerful representation mechanism. Extending ETL to extract templates that use dynamic features is an open problem.
2. Creation of a template selection procedure. It is necessary for the cases where too many templates are generated, such as in SRL. A straightforward method is to use only the templates extracted up to a given tree level, exactly as we have done for the CoNLL-2005 Corpus. However, other entropy guided template selection methods could be tested.
3. To speed up the ETL committee classification process. One possibility is to implement the Roche and Schabes [1] idea of converting transformation rules into deterministic finite-state transducers. According to Roche and Schabes, a transformation based English POS tagger converted into a finite-state tagger requires n steps to tag a sentence of length n, independently of the number of rules and the length of the context they require.
4. Investigation of other ensemble strategies.

References

1. Roche, E., Schabes, Y.: Deterministic part-of-speech tagging with finite-state transducers. Comput. Linguist. **21**(2), 227–253 (1995)
2. dos Santos, C.N., Oliveira, C.: Constrained atomic term: widening the reach of rule templates in transformation based learning. In: Portuguese Conference on Artificial Intelligence, EPIA, pp. 622–633 (2005)

Appendix A
ETL Committee Behavior

This appendix presents some results on the behavior of the ETL Committee learning strategy. We use the SRL CoNLL-2004 Corpus in all the experiments shown in this appendix. This corpus is described in Sect. 8.1. The development corpus is used to assess the system results.

This appendix is organized as follows. In Sect. A.1, we insvestigate the behavior of the ETL Committee performance as the ensemble size increases. In Sect. A.2, we analyze the ensemble performance sensitivity to the percentage of sampled features. In Sect. A.3, we insvestigate the contribution of redundant rules. In Sect. A.4, we examine the variance on the classification results due to the random nature of ETL Committee.

A.1 Ensemble Size

The *ensemble size* is defined by the number of boostrap samplings. Here, we examine how the ETL Committee performance behave as the number of committee members increases.

Figure A.1 demonstrates the relationship of the $F_{\beta=1}$ for a given number of ETL classifiers in the ensemble. We can see that the ensemble performance increases rapidly until approximately 40 classifiers are included. Then, the $F_{\beta=1}$ increases slowly until it gets stable with around 100 classifiers. Note that using just 50 models we have a $F_{\beta=1}$ of 68.7. ETL Committee has a similar behavior in the other three tasks: POS tagging, PCK and NER.

C. N. dos Santos and R. L. Milidiú, *Entropy Guided Transformation Learning: Algorithms and Applications*, SpringerBriefs in Computer Science, DOI: 10.1007/978-1-4471-2978-3, © The Author(s) 2012

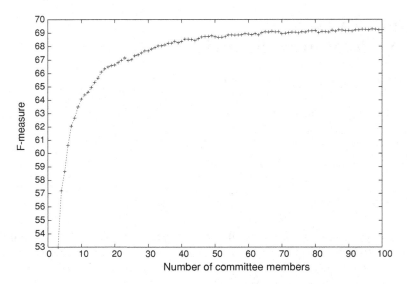

Fig. A.1 $F_{\beta=1}$ x Number of committee members curve

Table A.1 ETL Committee performance sensitivity to the percentage of sampled features

Percentage of sampled features (%)	Precision (%)	Recall (%)	$F_{\beta=1}$
100	75.43	61.95	68.03
90	75.97	62.21	68.40
80	76.40	62.32	68.65
70	76.44	**62.40**	**68.71**
60	76.52	61.87	68.42
50	**76.64**	61.50	68.24

A.2 Feature Sampling

The *feature sampling parameter* indicates the percentage of input features to be used in the training of each committee member. In this section, we insvestigate the ensemble performance sensitivity to the percentage of sampled features.

In Table A.1, we show the ETL Committee performance for different values of the feature sampling parameter. For this experiment, we create ensembles of 50 classifiers. The best performance occurs when 70% of the features are randomly sampled for each classifier. In this case, the $F_{\beta=1}$ increases by about 0.7 when compared to the result in the first table line, where all features are used. In Table A.1, we can see that even using only 50% of the features, the performance does not degrade. However, using less than 70% of the features can lead to poor results for tasks with a few number of features such as POS tagging and PCK.

Table A.2 Contribution of redundant rules for the ETL Committee performance

Redundant rules	Precision (%)	Recall (%)	$F_{\beta=1}$
YES	76.44	62.40	68.71
NO	76.63	59.10	66.73

Table A.3 Results of ten different ETL Committee runs

Run	Precision (%)	Recall (%)	$F_{\beta=1}$
1	75.80	62.14	68.29
2	76.02	62.03	68.31
3	75.97	62.21	68.40
4	76.18	62.13	68.44
5	76.33	62.17	68.53
6	76.34	62.17	68.53
7	76.30	62.23	68.55
8	76.47	62.15	68.57
9	76.27	62.31	68.59
10	76.66	62.12	68.63

A.3 Redundant Rules

In this section, we analyze the contribution of redundant rules for the ETL Committee performance. In Table A.2, we show the ETL Committee performance when redundant rules are used or not used. For this experiment, we create ensembles of 50. The result in the first table line corresponds to the default ETL Committee method, which uses redundant rules. The second table line presents the ensemble performance when redundant rules are not used. In this case, the $F_{\beta=1}$ drops by about two points. This finding indicates that the overfitting provided by redundant rules is very important to the construction of more diverse ETL classifiers. ETL Committee has a similar behavior in the other three tasks.

A.4 ETL Committee Random Nature

ETL Committee uses randomized methods to build diverse classifiers. Due to this random nature, the performance of two different ETL Committee models may vary, even if they are trained using exactly the same parameter setting. In this section, we investigate how the ETL Committee performance varies with different algorithm runs. We perform an experiment that consists in training ten different committees using the same parameter setting. Each committee contains 50 classifiers. We use the SRL CoNLL-2004 development set to assess the performance of each ensemble model.

In Table A.3, we show the ETL Committee performance for the ten different runs. The standard deviation of the F-score is 0.12. Since this value is very small, it can be concluded that the random nature of the learning algorithm has a little impact in the variance of the final result. The standard deviation is even smaller if we use a larger number of classifiers in the committee. In this experiment we use 50 classifies. However, we use ensembles of size 100 for the experiments shown in Chaps. 5, 6, 7 and 8. Therefore, the reported ETL Committee results are stable.